Basement *Home Plans*

Featuring 100 Homes That Grow With You

A Designs Direct Publishing Book

Presented by

Donald A. Gardner Architects, Inc.
150 Executive Center Drive, Suite 215
Greenville, SC 29615

Donald A. Gardner — CEO and Publisher
Angela Santerini — President
Dominic Foley — Publisher
Kathleen Nalley — Editor
Bishana Shipp — Graphic Artist
Jennifer Bacon — Writer

Contributing Illustrators
Architectural Art
Greg Havens
Barry Nathan

Contributing Photographers
Matthew Scott Photographer, Inc.
Photographic Solutions
Riley & Riley Photography, Inc.
Stephen Stinson Photography
Winward Photography

Cover photo by Matthew Scott Photographer, Inc. Charleston, SC
Printed by Toppan Printing Co., Hong Kong

First Printing, September 2005

10 9 8 7 6 5 4 3 2 1

Table of Contents

RITES *of* PASSAGE

It's a place where dreams come to life. It's where first love blossoms and bands practice. It's the space where pipe dreams become corporate realities, and families create memories that last for generations. Where is this oasis? It's the basement, and while it's only as good as the family that it surrounds, if finished and nurtured, it becomes a room where these memories and milestone moments are created.

While the upstairs, formal living areas are an important part of choosing a home plan, homebuyers often forget about the lower-level bonus that comes with many homes. Historically, basements were cold, damp, wet spaces that invited mold in

and kept family members out. Today, however, basements are complete home theaters, flourishing offices and fitness facilities.

Why not take advantage of the space a basement affords you? As a family grows and changes, versatility is important in a floor plan, and a basement provides the ultimate in additional square footage. Within this lower-level retreat, families can design a room that perfectly caters to their needs. Creating a space for your favorite hobby or pasttime not only reduces the hassle of leaving the house, but also saves you money!

In this book you'll find fresh ideas, complete with full-color photography, to bring your basement dreams to life! Because a home is a large and long-term investment, we understand every family needs a space that can grow with them. What was once a child's playroom can later function as a teenager's retreat, and finally as an adult game room. So get comfortable as you begin to explore the possibilities of a room down under.

While the plans in this book are meant to inspire you, the possibilities are limitless. We've divided this collection of favorite home plans into four, easy-to-read sections that describe our favorite uses for the basement. Whether you fancy a room to relax with your family, or you plan to turn your business idea into a full-fledged company, the basement is a cost-effective alternative to adding on to your home. No longer the scary place to hide the hot water heater or Grandma's sofa, your basement will quickly become the most lived-in room of your home.

Sections

✓ Leisure Locales
✓ Business Places
✓ Healthy Habitats
✓ Useful Spaces

✓ Leisure Locales

Leisure Locales provides direction for planning a recreation area. Home theaters, wine cellars and children's playrooms are all explored as we help you make the most of your underground rumpus room.

✓ Business Places

Business Places enables you to turn your career dreams into real-life possibilities. Whether you use the space for a small home office or a place to entertain clients, learn how to be the most productive in your basement office.

✓ Healthy Habitats

Healthy Habitats features plans and ideas to help you create a fitness area in your basement, year after year. From home gyms to climbing walls, these plans flex your fitness ideas for the basement.

✓ Useful Spaces

Useful Spaces includes plans to create an exciting place to hone a craft or mend the family's loose threads (or just do the laundry).

LEISURE

LOCALES

The most popular of all basement uses is for recreation. Most people spend the majority of their day working and looking after children, so the idea of work hard/play hard becomes an everyday philosophy. But often trying to find a way to "play" requires trips to the movies, restaurants or specialty locations that become expensive.

...Rec rooms for every interest

With DVD players as common as VCRs and similarly priced, turning the basement into a media room is an entertaining way to promote family time and save money. Take advantage of the lack of windows in most basements and turn it into a movie theater. By using heavy drapes and wooden floors, you can bring theater-quality sound to your favorite films. Big-screen televisions and projectors are popular devices for viewing movies, while installing a nearby kitchenette makes it a close step for popcorn and sodas.

Also popular for basements is a teenager's retreat. Give your son or daughter a place to "hang out" while you give yourself a rest from worrying about their whereabouts. Dart boards, billiards tables and pinball machines coupled with a few overstuffed chairs and couches make a great lounge. For older crowds, the use of the kitchenette goes well with a wet bar. Increasingly popular, the basement bar enables you to live out any dreams of owning your own watering hole. The darker environment lends itself naturally to the classic feel of an old tavern or wine-tasting room. Perfect for dark, cool places, wine cellars are also favorable in basements due to the problem of wine spoiling in warmer climates.

Whatever your preferred way to relax, the basement plans in this section work naturally to enable you to build your favorite getaway room. Take your shoes off, and enjoy the countless ways you'll be able to spend your free time.

© 1998 Donald A. Gardner Architects, Inc.

RUSTIC RETREAT

Above: The arched entryway and timeless wooden door mirror the natural look of the rich interior.

Left: Modified from the original plan, this home now includes a red galvanized metal roof for a striking exterior.

Above: A wall of windows and hipped cathedral ceiling highlight the master bedroom.

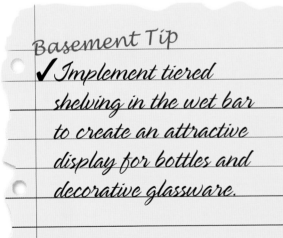

Basement Tip

✔ *Implement tiered shelving in the wet bar to create an attractive display for bottles and decorative glassware.*

A stunning center dormer with arched window and decorative wood brackets cap the entry to this extraordinary hillside estate. Floor-to-ceiling windows invite the natural light inside, while stable-style garage doors and a decorative clerestory window add extra curb appeal to the *Crowne Canyon*.

Exposed wood beams enhance the magnificent cathedral ceilings of the foyer, great room, dining room, master bedroom and screened porch, while ten-foot ceilings top the remainder of the first floor. The great

Above: Exposed wood beams and a stone fireplace bring natural elements into the great room.

room takes in scenic rear views through a wall of windows. Relaxing spaces are abundant as fireplaces add warmth and ambience to the great room, basement, screened porch and the master suite's study/sitting area.

The kitchen is complete with its center cooktop island, pantry and ample room for two or more cooks. A three-car garage allows space for storage or a golf cart, while a spacious screened porch allows three- to four-season enjoyment of the outdoors.

Ideal for a pool table, the expansive media/rec room also features a built-in wet bar that acts as a gathering place to interact with friends. Guests will enjoy the downstairs fireplace, outdoor access and convenience of the nearby

bedrooms and bathrooms, which become great guest-suites for overnight visitors or rooms for larger families. Two covered patios off the media/rec room are excellent places to convene outdoors when entertaining larger groups. With room to accommodate even the largest gatherings comfortably, this home contains the flexibility to change as your family grows.

Left: The spacious basement level provides plenty of room for a wet-bar and game room.

Above: With a rear wall of windows and outdoor living areas, this home captures the essence of Mother Nature.

Crowne Canyon

BHPDG01-732D

5 Bedroom, 4 Baths, 2 Half-Baths
First Floor.......... 3040 sq ft
Basement.......... <u>1736 sq ft</u>
Total Living......... 4776 sq ft
Width................. 106' 5"
Depth................. 104' 2"
Foundation...... Hillside
Walkout

1-800-388-7580

www.basementhomeplans.com

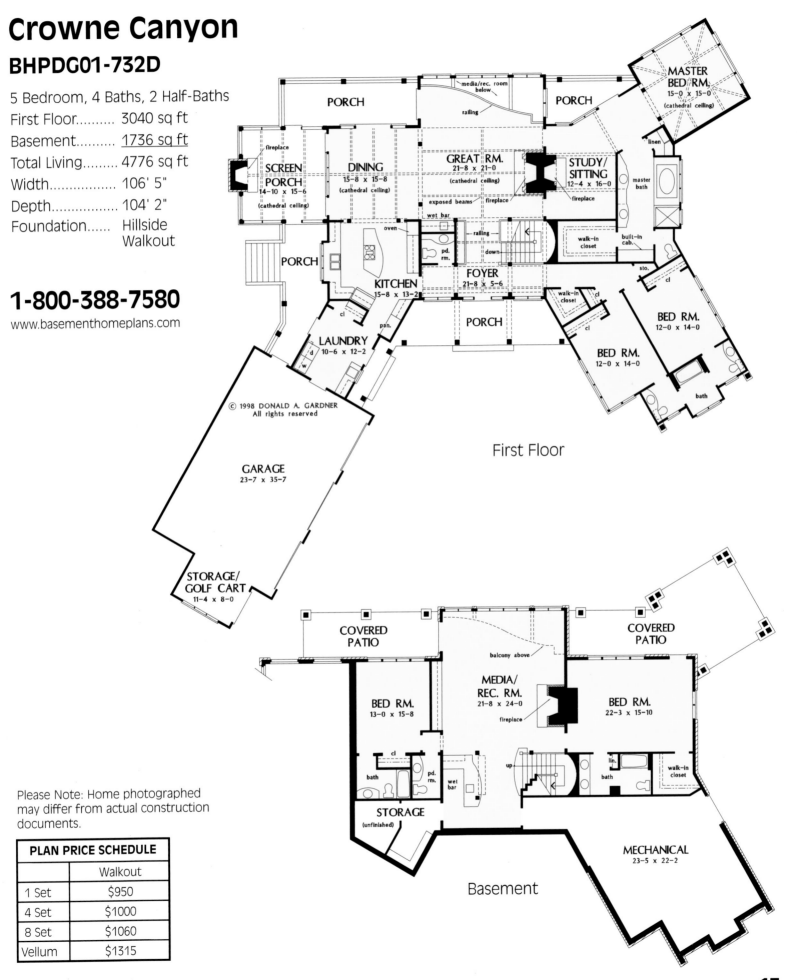

First Floor

Please Note: Home photographed
may differ from actual construction
documents.

Basement

PLAN PRICE SCHEDULE	
	Walkout
1 Set	$950
4 Set	$1000
8 Set	$1060
Vellum	$1315

© 1996 Donald A. Gardner Architects, I

COUNTRY CLASSIC

With a traditional farmhouse feel, the **Arbordale** encompasses prominent twin gables and a wraparound porch to create a welcoming entrance. The rear of the home is equally enchanting with a bay window and dual gables. To ensure privacy, the master bedroom is in an entire wing all to itself and features a walk-in closet for additional storage. The large master bath includes his-and-her sinks and separate shower, making morning rituals less hectic. Bay windows elegantly embrace the living and dining rooms, and the bonus room above the garage functions as an additional bedroom or playroom.

Above: Accented by striking columns, the living room ushers natural sunlight through the French doors and bay window.

Left: The wide rocking-chair front porch and symmetrical gables provide a classic, traditional look to this country farmhouse.

Left: The loft creates the ultimate relaxing space for reading on a sleepy Sunday afternoon.

The spacious kitchen overlooks the bayed breakfast area, and a convenient powder room is tucked away behind the kitchen.

An ultimate location for a home theater, the basement is punctuated by columns, which could help to define separate seating arrangements.

This two-story plan capitalizes on open living areas and provides abundant space for your creativity.

Below: Overlooking the rear porch, the breakfast room provides a calming view for family meals.

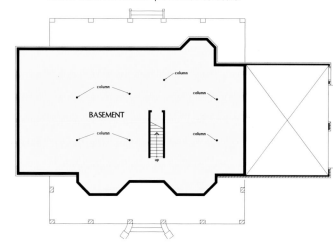

Rear Elevation

Basement

Above: As refined as the front exterior, the rear exterior features a large porch with ample space to watch late-afternoon sunsets.

$$\begin{array}{r} 2086 \\ 1077 \\ \hline 3163 \\ 403 \\ \hline 3566 \\ 2078 \\ \hline 5644 \end{array}$$

Arbordale
BHPDG01-452A

4 Bedroom, 3 1/2 Bath

First Floor.......... 2086 sq ft

Second Floor..... 1077 sq ft

Total Living.........3163 sq ft

Bonus................ 403 sq ft

Opt. Basement.. 2078 sq ft

Width................. 81' 10"

Depth.................51' 8"

Foundation...... Basement or Crawl Space

1-800-388-7580

www.basementhomeplans.com

Please Note: Home photographed may differ from actual construction documents.

PLAN PRICE SCHEDULE		
	Crawl	Basement
1 Set	$705	$980
4 Set	$755	$1,030
8 Set	$815	$1,090
Vellum	$1,055	$1,330

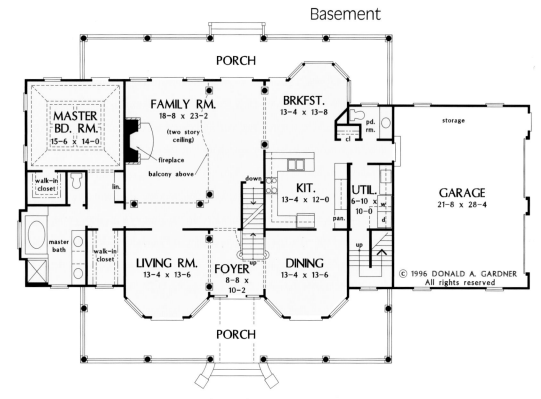

First Floor

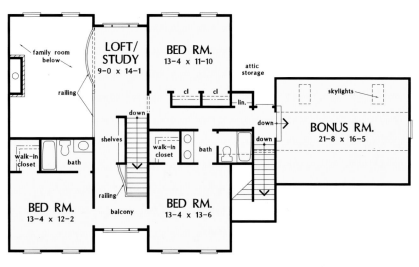

Second Floor

www.basementhomeplans.com

© 2002 Donald A. Gardner Architects, Inc.

NATURAL INSPIRATION

Basement Tip

✓ *Remember when storing wine in the downstairs wine cellar, use the bottom row for white and rose wines and higher/top rows for reds.*

High gables combine with columns for a stunning exterior on this Craftsman home. Ceiling treatments throughout the rooms create architectural interest and visual space, while built-ins in the great room add convenient storage to the *Satchwell*.

Custom molding and built-in shelves give the great room exciting extras.

Left: Stainless steel appliances stand out against sleek, hardwood floors and matching wooden cabinetry.

Right: A tray ceiling adds vertical volume, and a French door allows additional sunlight to flood through the master bedroom.

While a screened porch allows for comfortable outdoor entertaining, a bonus room lies near two secondary bedrooms and offers flexibility. The bedroom/study could function as a library or home office, with access to an adjacent full bath. Positioned for privacy, the master suite features access to the screened porch, dual walk-in closets and a well-appointed bath, including a private privy, garden tub, double vanity and spacious shower. The split-bedroom plan ensures ultimate privacy.

The basement level could make an ideal wine cellar, recreation area or guest quarters. For a family with teenagers, it could become an ideal "hangout" spot.

Rear Elevation

Above: A screened porch off the great room allows nature enthusiasts to comfortably spend time outside.

Note: Basement floor plans not to scale.

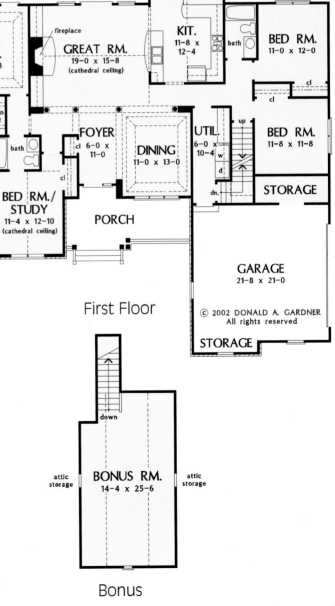

BASEMENT

column
column
column
up

Basement

Satchwell
BHPDG01-967A

4 Bedroom, 3 Bath

First Floor.......... <u>2117 sq ft</u>

Total Living........2117 sq ft

Bonus................ 406 sq ft

Opt. Basement.. 2180 sq ft

Width................ 64' 10"

Depth................ 64' 0"

Foundation...... Basement or Crawl Space

1-800-388-7580
www.basementhomeplans.com

Please Note: Home photographed may differ from actual construction documents.

PLAN PRICE SCHEDULE		
	Crawl	Basement
1 Set	$615	$865
4 Set	$665	$915
8 Set	$725	$975
Vellum	$925	$1,175

First Floor

SCREEN PORCH
25-10 x 9-4

BRKFST.
11-8 x 8-10
(cathedral ceiling)

KIT.
11-8 x 12-4

bath

BED RM.
11-0 x 12-0

cl
cl

MASTER BED RM.
16-2 x 13-8

fireplace

GREAT RM.
19-0 x 15-8
(cathedral ceiling)

walk-in closet

walk-in closet

master bath

bath

FOYER
cl 6-0 x 11-0

DINING
11-0 x 13-0

UTIL.
6-0 x 10-4

up

w
d

BED RM.
11-8 x 11-8

cl

dn.

STORAGE

BED RM./ STUDY
11-4 x 12-10
(cathedral ceiling)

PORCH

GARAGE
21-8 x 21-0

STORAGE

Bonus

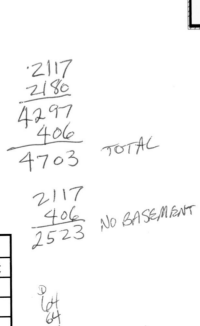

down

attic storage

BONUS RM.
14-4 x 25-6

attic storage

handwritten notes:
2117
2180
4297
406
4703 TOTAL

2117
406 NO BASEMENT
2523

64
64
64
64
286 linear feet

A covered porch and walkout basement combine with twin dormers to create an attractive rear exterior.

MODERN CHARACTER

Above: Perfect for an underground tavern, cocktail lounge or additional gathering area, the basement level is the ideal retreat.

Basement Tip

✓ By installing a nearby kitchenette, kids can quickly refuel on drinks and snacks without ever needing to come upstairs.

A low-maintenance exterior and unique floor plan make the *Peekskill* an attractive design that grows with your family. A combination of cedar-shake siding, stone and decorative brackets gives this home Craftsman charm. Front, rear and screened porches meld indoor and outdoor living.

Eating areas are abundant as the kitchen, dining and breakfast rooms all spill into one another. Opening into the great room, the kitchen features a serving bar to make quick meals a cinch.

A generous second level boasts two bedrooms, overlooking loft and large bonus room. Below, the basement walks out onto a covered patio and works well for an underground bar and game room.

With an alluring exterior and matching interior, the *Peekskill's* flexible floor plan is ideal for today's expanding families.

Above: A cathedral ceiling in the great room elegantly expands the height of the formal living area.

Right: Black appliances combined with dark cabinetry enrich the open kitchen.

Above: An oversized dormer and low-maintenance exterior create an exciting façade.

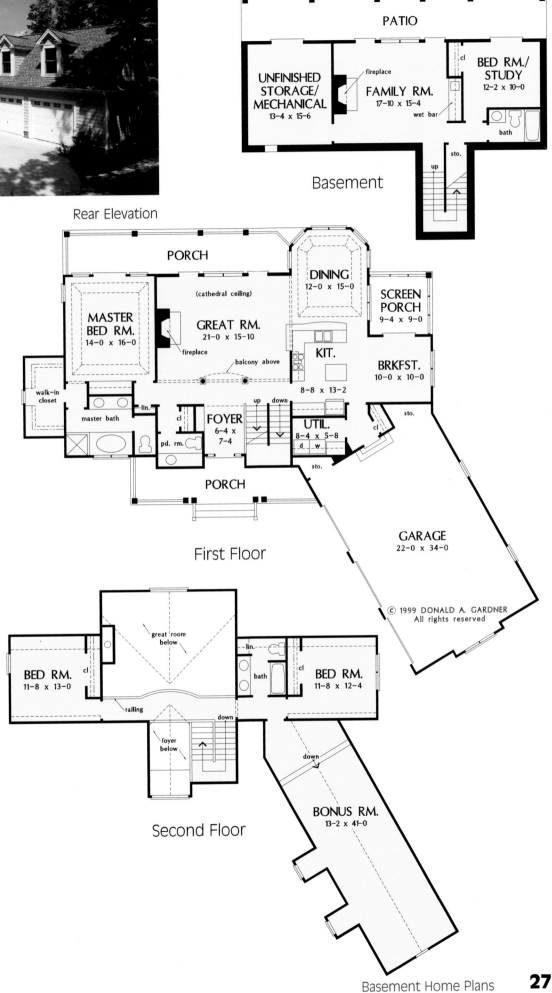

Basement

Rear Elevation

PATIO

UNFINISHED STORAGE/ MECHANICAL 13-4 x 15-6

fireplace

FAMILY RM. 17-10 x 15-4

wet bar

cl

BED RM./ STUDY 12-2 x 10-0

bath

sto.

up

PORCH

DINING 12-0 x 15-0

SCREEN PORCH 9-4 x 9-0

(cathedral ceiling)

MASTER BED RM. 14-0 x 16-0

GREAT RM. 21-0 x 15-10

fireplace

balcony above

KIT. 8-8 x 13-2

BRKFST. 10-0 x 10-0

walk-in closet

master bath

lin.

cl

up

down

FOYER 6-4 x 7-4

pd. rm.

UTIL. 8-4 x 5-8

d   w

cl

sto.

sto.

PORCH

First Floor

GARAGE 22-0 x 34-0

© 1999 DONALD A. GARDNER
All rights reserved

Peekskill
BHPDG01-780D

4 Bedroom, 3 1/2 Bath

First Floor.......... 1662 sq ft
Second Floor..... 585 sq ft
Basement.......... 706 sq ft
Total Living........ 2953 sq ft
Bonus............... 575 sq ft
Width................. 81' 4"
Depth................. 68' 8"
Foundation........ Hillside Walkout

1-800-388-7580
www.basementhomeplans.com

Please Note: Home photographed may differ from actual construction documents.

great room below

BED RM. 11-8 x 13-0

cl

lin.

bath

BED RM. 11-8 x 12-4

railing

down

foyer below

down

BONUS RM. 13-2 x 41-0

Second Floor

PLAN PRICE SCHEDULE	
	Walkout
1 Set	$660
4 Set	$710
8 Set	$770
Vellum	$990

www.basementhomeplans.com

Basement Home Plans

Donald A. Gardner Architects

Leisure Locales

Calhoun
BHPDG01-392A
1-800-388-7580

4 Bedroom, 2 1/2 Bath

First Floor..........	<u>2200 sq ft</u>
Total Living........	2200 sq ft
Bonus...............	491 sq ft
Opt. Basement..	2299 sq ft
Width..............	74'10"
Depth..............	55'8"
Foundation......	Basement or Crawl Space

PLAN PRICE SCHEDULE		
	Crawl	Basement
1 Set	$615	$865
4 Set	$665	$915
8 Set	$725	$975
Vellum	$925	$1,175

Rear Elevation

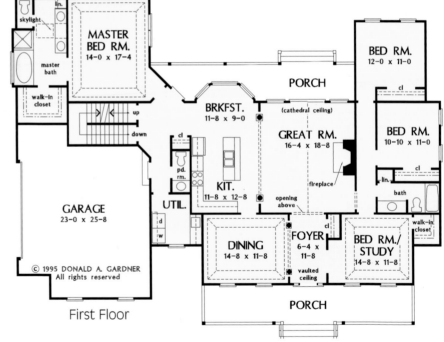

First Floor

Note: Basement floor plans not to scale.

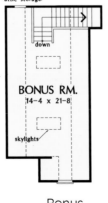

Bonus

Basement

www.basementhomeplans.com

Leisure Locales

© 2001 Donald A. Gardner, Inc.

Whiteheart
BHPDG01-926A
1-800-388-7580

3 Bedroom, 2 Bath

First Floor............. 2266 sq ft
Total Living........... 2266 sq ft
Opt. Basement..... 2351 sq ft
Width.................. 57'8"
Depth.................. 68'0"
Foundation........ Basement or Crawl Space

PLAN PRICE SCHEDULE		
	Crawl	Basement
1 Set	$615	$865
4 Set	$665	$915
8 Set	$725	$975
Vellum	$925	$1,175

Basement Tip

Use a dimmer to elegantly soften light during viewing time in your home theater.

Note: Basement floor plans not to scale.

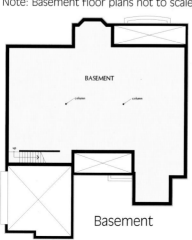

Basement

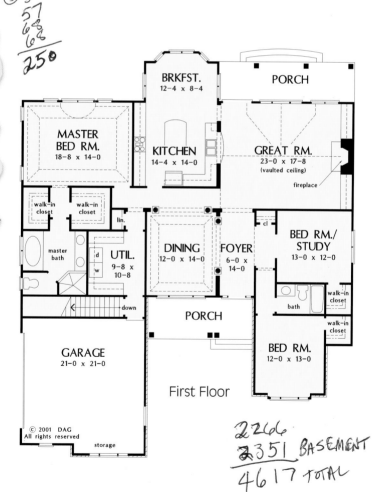

First Floor

Photographed home may have been modified from the original construction documents.

Rear Elevation

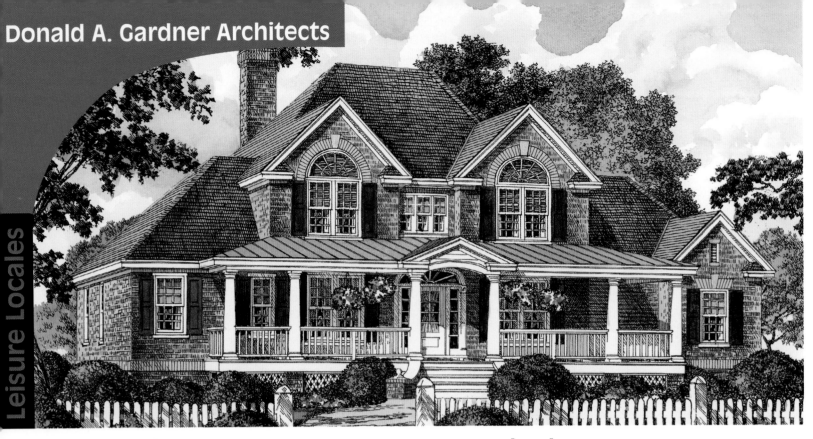

© 2003 Donald A. Gardner, Inc.

Peppermill
BHPDG01-1034A
1-800-388-7580

4 Bedroom, 3 1/2 Bath

First Floor............ 1809 sq ft
Second Floor........ <u>777 sq ft</u>
Total Living............2586 sq ft
Bonus...................264 sq ft
Opt. Basement..... 1809 sq ft
Width...................70'7"
Depth...................48'4"
Foundation..........Basement or Crawl Space

PLAN PRICE SCHEDULE		
	Crawl	Basement
1 Set	$660	$910
4 Set	$710	$960
8 Set	$770	$1,020
Vellum	$990	$1,240

Rear Elevation

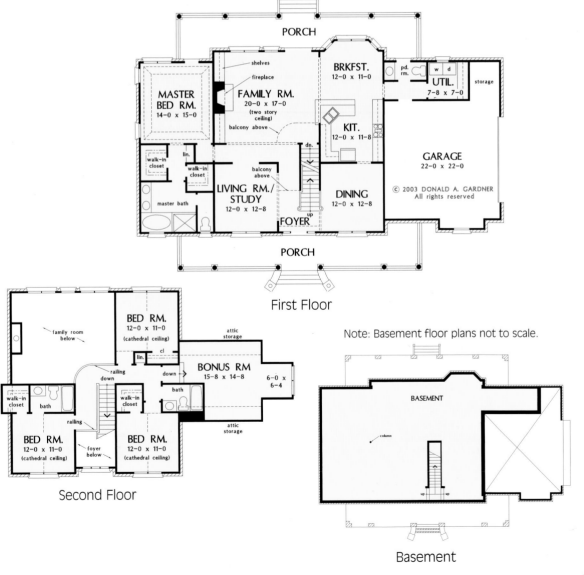

First Floor

Second Floor

Note: Basement floor plans not to scale.

Basement

Leisure Locales

Evergreen
BHPDG01-479D
1-800-388-7580

3 Bedroom, 2 Bath

First Floor..........	<u>1680 sq ft</u>
Total Living........	1680 sq ft
Basement..........	1653 sq ft
Width.................	62'8"
Depth.................	59'10"
Foundation........	Hillside Walkout

Note: Basement floor plans not to scale.

First Floor

Basement

PLAN PRICE SCHEDULE	
	Walkout
1 Set	$570
4 Set	$620
8 Set	$680
Vellum	$860

GARAGE
22-0 x 22-0

Rear Elevation

© 2003 Donald A. Gardner, Inc.

Questling
BHPDG01-1004D
1-800-388-7580

4 Bedroom, 4 Bath
First Floor..........1938 sq ft
Basement..........1033 sq ft
Total Living........2971 sq ft
Width................77'6"
Depth................42'7"
Foundation........Hillside
                       Walkout

PLAN PRICE SCHEDULE	
	Walkout
1 Set	$660
4 Set	$710
8 Set	$770
Vellum	$990

Rear Elevation

Basement

First Floor

www.basementhomeplans.com

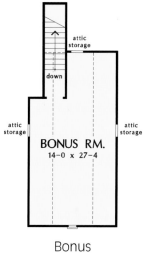

Bonus

Note: Basement floor plans not to scale.

Basement

First Floor

© 2003 Donald A. Gardner, Inc.

Edelweiss
BHPDG01-1013A
1-800-388-7580

3 Bedroom, 2 Bath
First Floor.......... 2039 sq ft
Total Living......... 2039 sq ft
Bonus............... 361 sq ft
Opt. Basement..... 2062 sq ft
Width................ 54'8"
Depth................ 73'4"
Foundation........ Basement or Crawl Space

PLAN PRICE SCHEDULE		
	Crawl	Basement
1 Set	$570	$795
4 Set	$620	$845
8 Set	$680	$905
Vellum	$860	$1085

Rear Elevation

Hollingbourne
BHPDG01-990A
1-800-388-7580

5 Bedroom, 4 1/2 Bath

First Floor..........	2072 sq ft
Second Floor.....	1279 sq ft
Total Living........	3351 sq ft
Bonus................	386 sq ft
Opt. Basement.....	2118 sq ft
Width.................	73'8"
Depth..................	50'0"
Foundation..........	Basement or Crawl Space

PLAN PRICE SCHEDULE		
	Crawl	Basement
1 Set	$705	$980
4 Set	$755	$1,030
8 Set	$815	$1,090
Vellum	$1,055	$1,330

Rear Elevation

First Floor

Second Floor

Note: Basement floor plans not to scale.

Basement

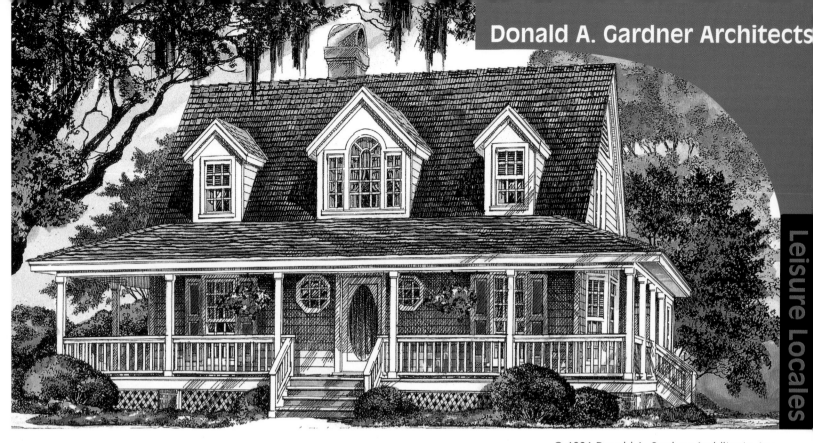

Morninglory
BHPDG01-236A
1-800-388-7580

3 Bedroom, 2 1/2 Bath

First Floor........... 1325 sq ft
Second Floor...... <u>453 sq ft</u>
Total Living......... 1778 sq ft
Opt. Basement.. 1311 sq ft
Width................. 48'4"
Depth................. 40'8"
Foundation....... Basement or Crawl Space

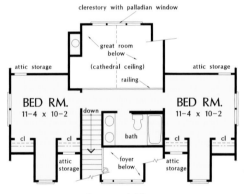

Second Floor

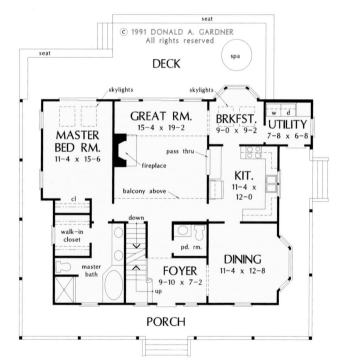

First Floor

PLAN PRICE SCHEDULE		
	Crawl	Basement
1 Set	$570	$795
4 Set	$620	$845
8 Set	$680	$905
Vellum	$860	$1085

Note: Basement floor plans not to scale.

Basement

Rear Elevation

Brennan
BHPDG01-350A
1-800-388-7580

3 Bedroom, 2 Bath

First Floor.......... <u>1752 sq ft</u>
Total Living........ 1752 sq ft
Opt. Basement.. 1825 sq ft
Width................ 69'6"
Depth................ 59'8"
Foundation........ Basement or
Crawl Space

PLAN PRICE SCHEDULE		
	Crawl	Basement
1 Set	$570	$795
4 Set	$620	$845
8 Set	$680	$905
Vellum	$860	$1085

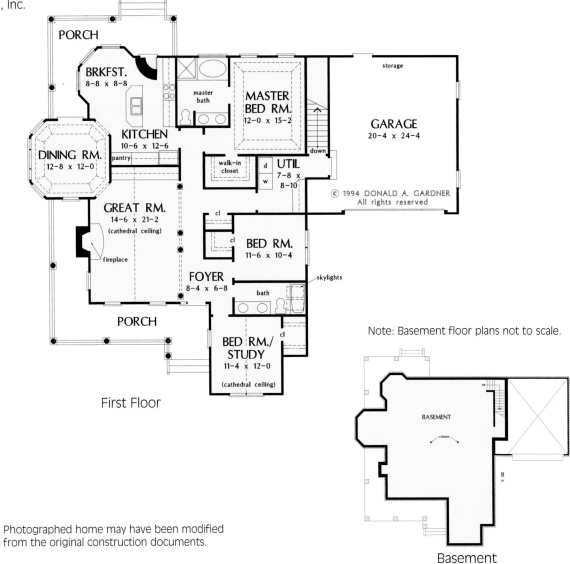

PORCH

BRKFST.
8-8 x 8-8

master bath

MASTER BED RM.
12-0 x 15-2

storage

GARAGE
20-4 x 24-4

KITCHEN
10-6 x 12-6

DINING RM.
12-8 x 12-0

pantry

walk-in closet

down

UTIL
7-8 x
8-10

d w

GREAT RM.
14-6 x 21-2
(cathedral ceiling)

cl

BED RM.
11-6 x 10-4

cl

fireplace

FOYER
8-4 x 6-8

skylights

bath

PORCH

BED RM./
STUDY
11-4 x 12-0

(cathedral ceiling)

First Floor

Note: Basement floor plans not to scale.

BASEMENT

column

Basement

Rear Elevation

Photographed home may have been modified
from the original construction documents.

Jamestowne
BHPDG01-828A
1-800-388-7580

4 Bedroom, 2 1/2 Bath

First Floor	1687 sq ft
Second Floor	821 sq ft
Total Living	2508 sq ft
Opt. Basement	1687 sq ft
Width	52'8"
Depth	72'4"
Foundation	Basement or Crawl Space

Second Floor

BED RM.
11-4 x 12-8

BED RM.
12-0 x 12-0

BED RM.
12-8 x 11-0

great room below

attic storage

railing

cl

bath

lin.

down

foyer below

attic storage

cl

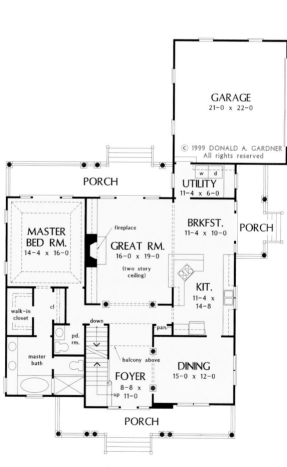

First Floor

GARAGE
21-0 x 22-0

PORCH

UTILITY
11-4 x 6-0

w d

MASTER BED RM.
14-4 x 16-0

fireplace

GREAT RM.
16-0 x 19-0

(two story ceiling)

BRKFST.
11-4 x 10-0

PORCH

KIT.
11-4 x 14-8

walk-in closet

cl

pd. rm.

master bath

down

pan.

balcony above

FOYER
8-8 x up 11-0

DINING
15-0 x 12-0

PORCH

PLAN PRICE SCHEDULE

	Crawl	Basement
1 Set	$660	$910
4 Set	$710	$960
8 Set	$770	$1,020
Vellum	$990	$1,240

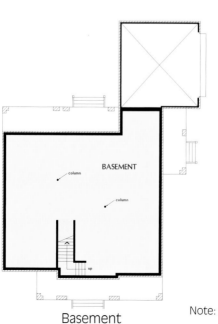

BASEMENT

column

column

up

Basement

Note: Basement floor plans not to scale.

Rear Elevation

© 2002 Donald A. Gardner, Inc.

Applemoor
BHPDG01-970A
1-800-388-7580

4 Bedroom, 3 Bath

First Floor............. <u>1961 sq ft</u>

Total Living........... 1961 sq ft

Bonus.................... 390 sq ft

Opt. Basement...... 2060 sq ft

Width.................... 50'0"

Depth.................... 63'8"

Foundation.......... Basement or Crawl Space

PLAN PRICE SCHEDULE		
	Crawl	Basement
1 Set	$570	$795
4 Set	$620	$845
8 Set	$680	$905
Vellum	$860	$1085

Rear Elevation

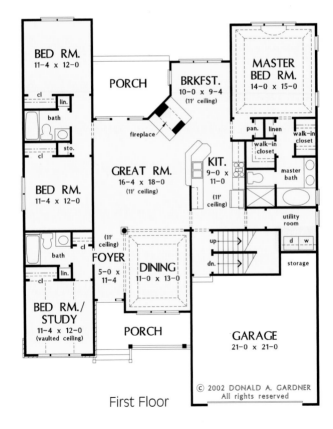

First Floor

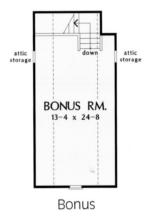

Bonus

Note: Basement floor plans not to scale.

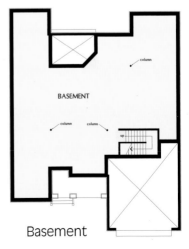

Basement

Basement Tip

Basement dark rooms are perfect for the avid photographer. Take advantage of the naturally dark space for developing film and enlarging prints.

Note: Basement floor plans not to scale.

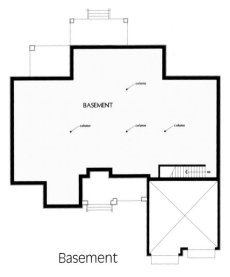

Basement

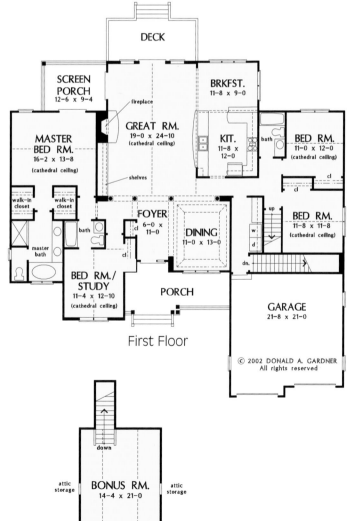

First Floor

DECK

SCREEN PORCH 12-6 x 9-4

GREAT RM. 19-0 x 24-10 (cathedral ceiling)

BRKFST. 11-8 x 9-0

KIT. 11-8 x 12-0

MASTER BED RM. 16-2 x 13-8 (cathedral ceiling)

BED RM. 11-0 x 12-0 (cathedral ceiling)

walk-in closet | walk-in closet

master bath | bath

FOYER 6-0 x 11-0

DINING 11-0 x 13-0

BED RM. 11-8 x 11-8 (cathedral ceiling)

BED RM./ STUDY 11-4 x 12-10 (cathedral ceiling)

PORCH

GARAGE 21-8 x 21-0

BONUS RM. 14-4 x 21-0

attic storage | attic storage

down

Bonus

Zimmerman
BHPDG01-987A
1-800-388-7580

4 Bedroom, 3 Bath
First Floor.............2272 sq ft
Total Living...........2272 sq ft
Bonus..................397 sq ft
Opt. Basement......2382 sq ft
Width....................64'10"
Depth....................63'2"
Foundation..........Basement or Crawl Space

PLAN PRICE SCHEDULE

	Crawl	Basement
1 Set	$615	$865
4 Set	$665	$915
8 Set	$725	$975
Vellum	$925	$1,175

Rear Elevation

© 2003 Donald A. Gardner, Inc.

Nicholson
BHPDG01-1021A
1-800-388-7580

3 Bedroom, 2 Bath

First Floor	1499 sq ft
Total Living	1499 sq ft
Bonus	393 sq ft
Opt. Basement	1606 sq ft
Width	52'3"
Depth	50'0"
Foundation	Basement or Crawl Space

PLAN PRICE SCHEDULE		
	Crawl	Basement
1 Set	$525	$750
4 Set	$575	$800
8 Set	$635	$860
Vellum	$795	$1,020

Rear Elevation

First Floor

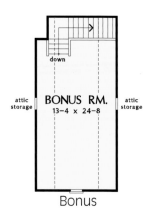

Bonus

Note: Basement floor plans not to scale.

Basement

Leisure Locales

© 2003 Donald A. Gardner, Inc.

Derbyville
BHPDG01-1032A
1-800-388-7580

4 Bedroom, 3 Bath

First Floor............. 1778 sq ft
Second Floor........ 498 sq ft
Total Living........... 2276 sq ft
Bonus.................. 315 sq ft
Opt. Basement..... 1778 sq ft
Width.................... 54'8"
Depth.................... 53'2"
Foundation.......... Basement or Crawl Space

Handwritten notes:
```
1778
 498
2276
$315  BONUS
2591  NO BASEMENT
1778
4379  TOTAL
```
```
① 54
  54
  53
  53
  214
```

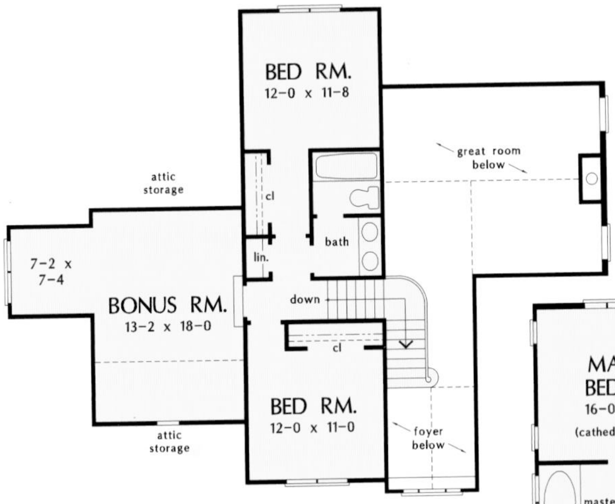

Second Floor

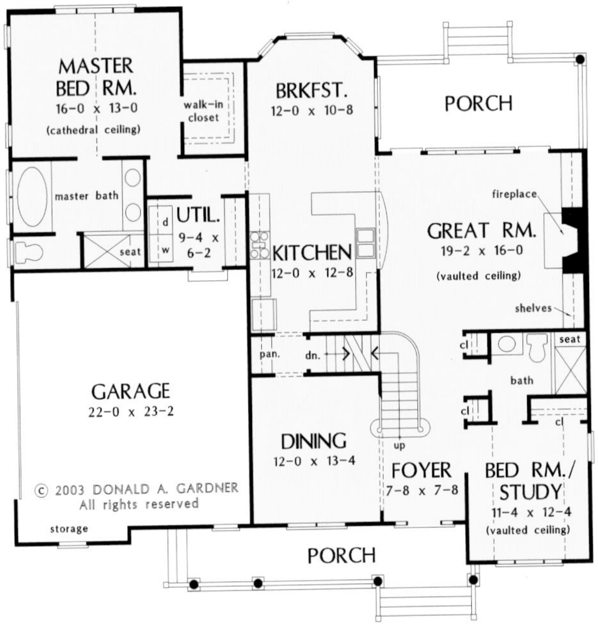

BED RM.
12-0 x 11-8

attic storage

7-2 x 7-4

BONUS RM.
13-2 x 18-0

attic storage

great room below

cl

bath

lin.

down

cl

BED RM.
12-0 x 11-0

foyer below

Note: Basement floor plans not to scale.

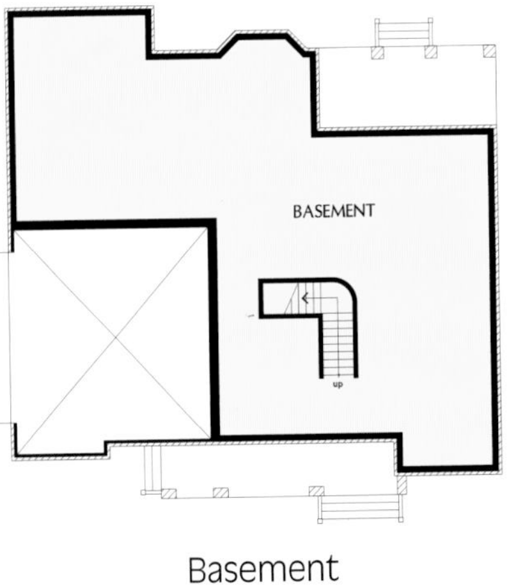

BASEMENT

Basement

MASTER BED RM.
16-0 x 13-0
(cathedral ceiling)

walk-in closet

master bath

seat

UTIL.
9-4 x 6-2

d w

KITCHEN
12-0 x 12-8

BRKFST.
12-0 x 10-8

PORCH

fireplace

GREAT RM.
19-2 x 16-0
(vaulted ceiling)

shelves

pan.   dn.

cl

bath

seat

GARAGE
22-0 x 23-2

DINING
12-0 x 13-4

FOYER
7-8 x 7-8

up

BED RM./ STUDY
11-4 x 12-4
(vaulted ceiling)

cl

cl

storage

© 2003 DONALD A. GARDNER
All rights reserved

PORCH

First Floor

PLAN PRICE SCHEDULE		
	Crawl	Basement
1 Set	$615	$865
4 Set	$665	$915
8 Set	$725	$975
Vellum	$925	$1,175

Rear Elevation

Basement Home Plans   **41**

© 2003 Donald A. Gardner, Inc.

Franklin
BHPDG01-1024A
1-800-388-7580

4 Bedroom, 2 Bath

First Floor.............. 2214 sq ft
Total Living........... 2214 sq ft
Bonus.................... 383 sq ft
Opt. Basement......2273 sq ft
Width.................... 60'4"
Depth.................... 70'0"
Foundation.......... Basement or
Crawl Space

PLAN PRICE SCHEDULE		
	Crawl	Basement
1 Set	$615	$865
4 Set	$665	$915
8 Set	$725	$975
Vellum	$925	$1,175

First Floor

First Floor rooms:
MASTER BED RM. 14-0 x 15-0 (vaulted ceiling)
walk-in closet
lin.
cl
seat
master bath
BRKFST. 9-8 x 9-10
KITCHEN 12-0 x 14-10
pantry
PORCH
wet bar
shelves
fireplace
GREAT RM. 20-0 x 16-4 (cathedral ceiling)
BED RM. 11-8 x 12-0
cl
cl
BED RM./ STUDY 11-0 x 12-0
bath
UTILITY 7-8 x 7-0
d w
storage
DINING 13-0 x 11-0
FOYER 6-4 x 11-0
cl
PORCH
BED RM. 11-0 x 12-0 (vaulted ceiling)
GARAGE 22-0 x 22-0
storage

Basement Tip

For home theaters, the distance between first-row seating and the screen should be two to three times the screen's diagonal measurement.

Note: Basement floor plans not to scale.

BASEMENT
column
column
column

Basement

Bonus:
attic storage
dn.
attic storage
BONUS RM. 14-4 x 25-8

Bonus

Rear Elevation

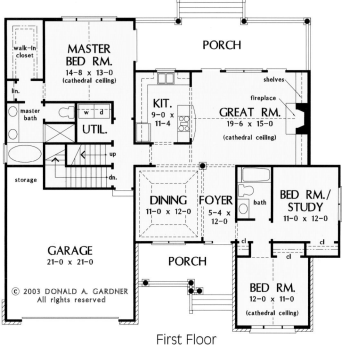

© 2003 Donald A. Gardner, Inc.

Greensboro
BHPDG01-1029A
1-800-388-7580

3 Bedroom, 2 Bath

First Floor	1644 sq ft
Total Living	1644 sq ft
Bonus	352 sq ft
Opt Basement	1692 sq ft
Width	56'0"
Depth	50'4"
Foundation	Basement or Crawl Space

First Floor

PLAN PRICE SCHEDULE

	Crawl	Basement
1 Set	$570	$795
4 Set	$620	$845
8 Set	$680	$905
Vellum	$860	$1085

Note: Basement floor plans not to scale.

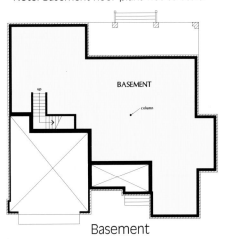

Basement

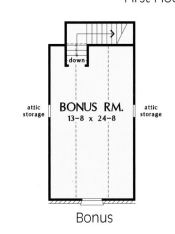

Bonus

Rear Elevation

BUSINESS PLACES

Many great companies started in the basement, and working from home is becoming increasingly popular. There is more to a home office, however, than a computer and filing cabinet. Whether your job requires clients to visit or you prefer a private area in which to work, the basement provides an ideal location for a home office.

Outline your wants and needs before you begin the construction process. Remember, the purpose of a home office is to save you time and money. If your home office doesn't work for you, it's doubtful you'll work in it.

...Work from home

Choose your location wisely. If you have the luxury of a door to the outside and plan to invite clients in, set up a waiting area near the door. Center your office around a window, if applicable, to illuminate the room with natural sunlight, and arrange your desk so that it faces the door to create an inviting environment for both you and your clients. You'll also want to position your office in an area that is not heavily traveled by other family members.

Take advantage of the open space and build an office that promotes productivity. This is your chance to work like a top-level executive and get out of the cubicle. Rich wood and warm colors create a soothing environment, while a good chair will keep you comfortable. Built-in desks and cabinetry look great and replace boring, gray file cabinets.

If you're expecting clients, you'll want an office that can comfortably seat two to three people, as well as a waiting area that implies you are professional. If you install a basement-level bathroom, it should be treated like an office restroom. Clients might feel uncomfortable in a bathroom that looks like it belongs upstairs, so choose neutral colors and modest decorations.

If you're sick of commuting or ready to turn your small idea into a full-fledged business, these basement plans are just the beginning for an impressive workspace.

© 2003 Allora, LLC

RURAL ENLIGHTENMENT

Above: The stone fireplace and cathedral ceiling add flair and volume to the great room.

Left: Stone columns on the basement level add to the impressive Arts-n-Crafts rear façade.

Above: Bright colors create a bold look in this modern kitchen with a generous center island.

Basement Tip

✔ *Install a separate office phone number with formal answering service to portray a professional appearance.*

Stone and cedar shake combine with triumphant gables and graceful arches to create a Craftsman exterior with European flair. Influenced by the cottages of old, the **Dogwood Ridge** boasts a rear wall of glasswork on both floors to capture breathtaking views, while rear and screened porches take living outdoors.

The sleek keeping room is hugged by a bay window, adding additional space to enjoy family meals.

The open floor plan distinguishes rooms by ceiling treatments and columns instead of enclosing space with walls. For added convenience and future planning, an elevator makes living easier. Custom features include a walk-in pantry, abundant storage space and large utility room with sink.

The master bedroom is complete with two walk-in closets, a double vanity, garden tub, separate shower and private privy. Along with the master suite, the secondary bedrooms take advantage of the natural scenery.

The basement level contains a multitude of home-office options, with two secondary bedrooms and a large rec room. With an optional guestroom and bath, this area is ideal for those who must entertain or meet with clients in their daily work. The separate entrance to the guestroom could function as a waiting area, complete with adjacent bathroom.

Left: Multiple rooms access the covered porch through French doors, allowing natural sunlight to flow through.

Left: A tray ceiling and bay window increase volume in the master bedroom.

Storage rooms are abundant throughout the lower level, allowing ample space for larger items. With two separate baths, the basement-level bedrooms have complete privacy.

A large keeping area rests just off the kitchen and both are augmented by cathedral ceilings. The elegant dining room flows naturally off the kitchen and into the great room, embracing the open floor plan. Accented by columns, the great and dining rooms naturally spill into one another, enabling a quick step from one room to the next.

Above: French doors and decorative windows illuminate the basement level.

The *Dogwood Ridge* is perfect for those who love entertaining outdoors or relaxing on a sunny afternoon. Featuring a screened porch, larger rear porch and covered patio below, you can embrace Mother Nature throughout the year .

Below: The extraordinary exterior boasts lavish curb appeal with a Craftsman façade, metal roof and stable-style garage doors.

© 2003 Allora, LLC

Dogwood Ridge

BHPAL01-5005

3 Bedroom, 3 1/2 Bath
First Floor......... 2090 sq ft
Basement......... 1111 sq ft
Total Living....... 3201 sq ft
Width.............. 71' 1"
Depth.............. 78' 6
Foundation...... Hillside
              Walkout

1-800-388-7580

www.basementhomeplans.com

Please Note: Home photographed may differ from actual construction documents.

PLAN PRICE SCHEDULE	
	Walkout
Vellum	Call for custom pricing

First Floor

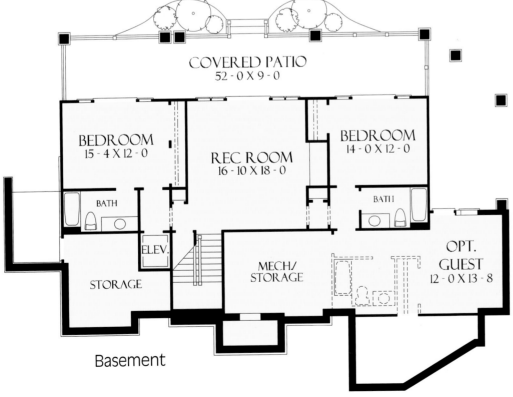

Basement

The Palladian window encased in the single large dormer above the porch gives the home a striking entrance.

© 1994 Donald A. Gardner Architects, Inc.

COMFORT CALLS

Custom molding around the fireplace and ceiling creates a dramatic look in the great room.

Restrained elegance inside and out characterizes the **Milford** with a dynamic, open floor plan. Elegant columns separate the large great room with cathedral ceiling from the kitchen with sky-lit breakfast area. The great room is strategically located in the middle of the house, assuring a central locale for family gatherings.

White cabinetry and appliances create a fluid and sleek look in the kitchen.

Tucked away for privacy, the master suite is a grand getaway. Homeowners will enjoy the well-appointed bath with corner whirlpool tub, separate shower and double-bowl vanity. The front bedroom can also be used as a study, while a bonus room over the garage adds flexibility.

The basement provides a chance to live like an executive and design the office you always wanted. With columns located strategically for room definition, a perfect office with seating area can be created. Or, divide the lower level into several rooms for husbands and wives who both work from home.

Above: Skylights allow natural light to flow freely throughout the breakfast room.

handwritten:
2651
447
—————
3098   NO BASEMENT
2764
—————
5762   TOTAL

① 63
63
82
82
—————
290

Rear Elevation

Milford

BHPDG01-331A

4 Bedroom, 2 1/2 Bath

First Floor.......... <u>2651 sq ft</u>

Total Living.........2651 sq ft

Bonus................ 447 sq ft

Opt. Basement.. 2764 sq ft

Width................. 63' 1"

Depth................ 82' 7"

Foundation...... Basement or Crawl Space

1-800-388-7580

www.basementhomeplans.com

Please Note: Home photographed may differ from actual construction documents.

PLAN PRICE SCHEDULE		
	Crawl	Basement
1 Set	$660	$910
4 Set	$710	$960
8 Set	$770	$1,020
Vellum	$990	$1,240

Basement

First Floor

Bonus

© 2001 Donald A. Gardner, Inc.

TRANQUIL LIVING

The *Yankton* takes a little of the Southeastern style and shares it with the rest of the nation's regions. By featuring an extraordinary low-maintenance exterior, twin dormers that separate two sets of matching gables, and a metal roof accenting the study's exterior window, this home emits maximum curb appeal.

Above: Multiple windows with decorative transoms brighten the dining room with natural sunlight.

Left: While the plan calls for brick, this homebuilder chose to use stone, creating a strong Craftsman exterior.

Basement Tip

✓ *Plan ahead and install plenty of electrical outlets to accommodate a fax, computer and future equipment to increase productivity as your company grows.*

Left: Wooden French doors elegantly coincide with the rustic interior of the great room.

Columns are used to define the dining room without enclosing space. Ceiling treatments give vertical volume to the master bath, bedroom and secondary bedroom. A convenient pass-thru connects the kitchen to the great room, and the fireplace has built-in shelves on both sides. A sizable utility room is complete with counter space and the garage features not one, but two, storage areas.

The open basement is a fitting location for a start-up business. With ample space for computer equipment, a sturdy desk and sitting area to brainstorm, this home's basement could be the place to turn a career dream into reality.

Below: A kitchen pass-thru enables stimulating views while washing dishes or preparing meals.

Above: Enjoying the outdoors is no problem with this impressive rear exterior.

Rear Elevation

Note: Basement floor plans not to scale.

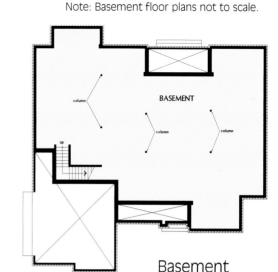

Basement

Yankton
BHPDG01-933A

3 Bedroom, 2 1/2 Bath

First Floor.......... <u>2344 sq ft</u>

Total Living.........2344 sq ft

Bonus............... 417 sq ft

Opt. Basement.. 2456 sq ft

Width................ 62' 3"

Depth................ 64' 2"

Foundation........Basement or Crawl Space

1-800-388-7580
www.basementhomeplans.com

Please Note: Home photographed may differ from actual construction documents.

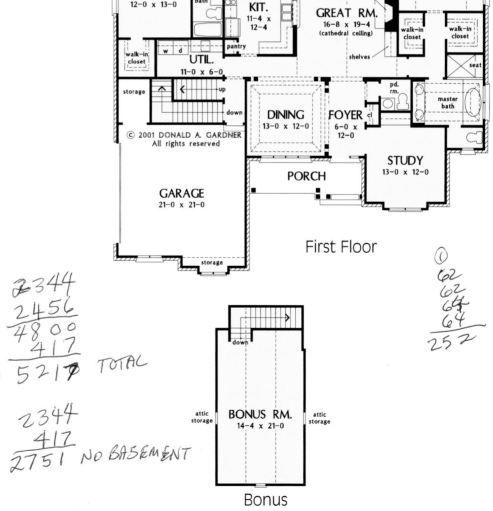

First Floor

Bonus

PLAN PRICE SCHEDULE		
	Crawl	Basement
1 Set	$615	$865
4 Set	$665	$915
8 Set	$725	$975
Vellum	$925	$1,175

Handwritten notes:
2344
2456
4800
417
521? TOTAL

2344
417
2751 NO BASEMENT

①
62
62
64
64
252

© 1999 Donald A. Gardner, Inc.

SERENE SETTING

This Craftsman-style home embraces the outdoors with its deck and patio. Featuring a cathedral ceiling in the great room, a fireplace with built-in cabinets and shelves, and a generous rear deck, the *Heathridge* includes plenty of extras.

The master suite boasts a tray ceiling, deck access, dual walk-in closets and an extravagant bath. A second master bedroom is located on the opposite side of the house and enjoys its own private bath, tray ceiling and deck access.

✓ Dressing in business-casual attire will help you achieve the work-place mindset, even if you are in your home. You never know when clients might stop by!

Above: Accented by transoms and a Palladian window, the great room's wall of windows provides ample opportunity for sunset views.

Left: Perfect as a mountain weekend home, this low-maintenance exterior with a convenient garage is a relaxing getaway retreat.

The basement level includes a spacious area in which to build a home office. A second fireplace lends itself nicely to enhance the room for meetings or entertaining clients, and the additional bedroom functions as a private office. The storage/mechanical area could be finished off, creating additional space on the lower level.

Above: A neutral-colored tile backsplash and rich wooden cabinetry contribute to the home's rustic feel.

Right: A generous rear deck creates an abundant space for weekend entertaining.

Rear Elevation

Above: Featuring both a covered patio and spacious rear deck, this home was designed for those who love to entertain.

Heathridge

BHPDG01-763D

3 Bedroom, 3 1/2 Bath

First Floor..........	2068 sq ft
Basement.........	930 sq ft
Total Living.........	2998 sq ft
Width.................	72' 4"
Depth.................	66' 0"
Foundation......	Hillside Walkout

1-800-388-7580

www.basementhomeplans.com

Please Note: Home photographed may differ from actual construction documents.

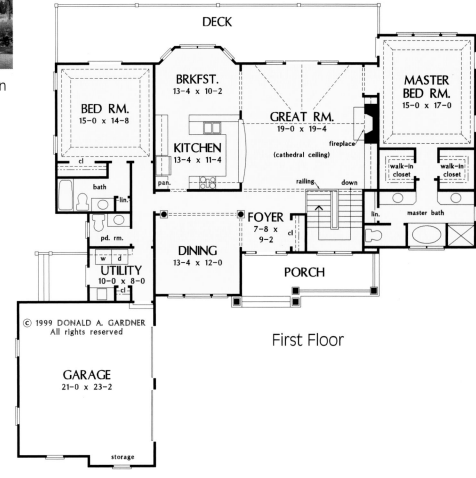

DECK

BRKFST.
13-4 x 10-2

BED RM.
15-0 x 14-8

GREAT RM.
19-0 x 19-4

MASTER BED RM.
15-0 x 17-0

cl

KITCHEN
13-4 x 11-4

(cathedral ceiling)

fireplace

bath

lin.

pan.

railing   down

walk-in closet   walk-in closet

pd. rm.

FOYER
7-8 x 9-2

cl

lin.   master bath

w   d

UTILITY
10-0 x 8-0

DINING
13-4 x 12-0

PORCH

cl

GARAGE
21-0 x 23-2

First Floor

storage

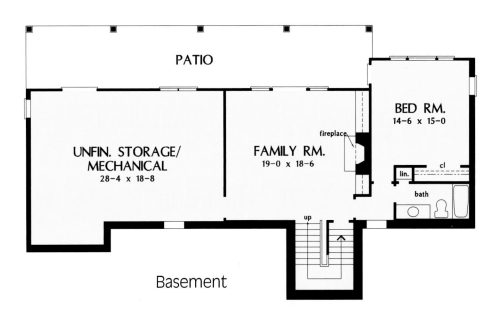

PATIO

UNFIN. STORAGE/ MECHANICAL
28-4 x 18-8

FAMILY RM.
19-0 x 18-6

fireplace

BED RM.
14-6 x 15-0

cl

lin.

bath

up

Basement

Business Places

© 1993 Donald A. Gardner Architects, Inc.

Burgess
BHPDG01-290A
1-800-388-7580

3 Bedroom, 2 1/2 Bath

First Floor............. 1618 sq ft
2nd floor.............. 570 sq ft
Total Living.......... 2188 sq ft
Bonus.................. 495 sq ft
Opt. Basement..... 1618 sq ft
Width.................. 54'0"
Depth.................. 49'0"
Foundation......... Basement or
　　　　　　　　　　Crawl Space

PLAN PRICE SCHEDULE		
	Crawl	Basement
1 Set	$615	$865
4 Set	$665	$915
8 Set	$725	$975
Vellum	$925	$1,175

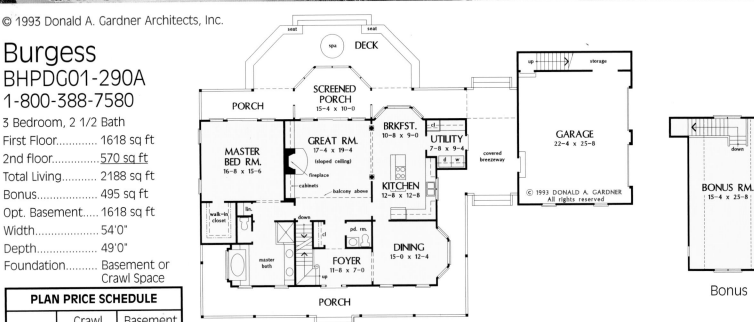

First Floor

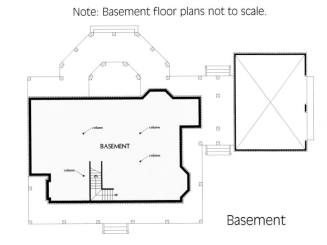

Note: Basement floor plans not to scale.

Bonus

Second Floor

Basement

Rear Elevation

Business Places

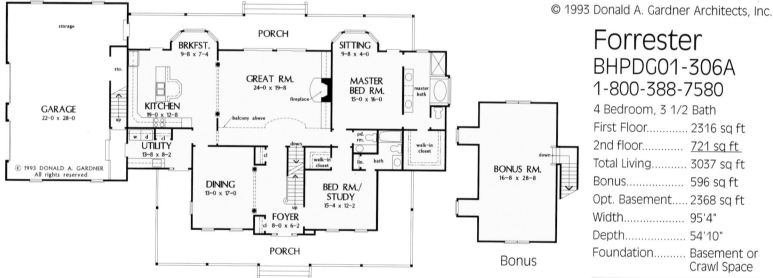

© 1993 Donald A. Gardner Architects, Inc.

Forrester
BHPDG01-306A
1-800-388-7580

4 Bedroom, 3 1/2 Bath

First Floor	2316 sq ft
2nd floor	721 sq ft
Total Living	3037 sq ft
Bonus	596 sq ft
Opt. Basement	2368 sq ft
Width	95'4"
Depth	54'10"
Foundation	Basement or Crawl Space

First Floor

Bonus

Photographed home may have been modified from the original construction documents.

Note: Basement floor plans not to scale.

PLAN PRICE SCHEDULE

	Crawl	Basement
1 Set	$705	$980
4 Set	$755	$1,030
8 Set	$815	$1,090
Vellum	$1055	$1,330

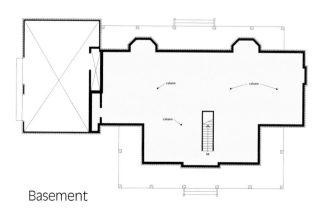

Basement

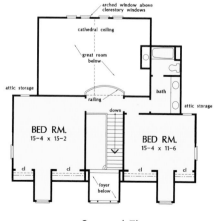

Second Floor

Rear Elevation

Business Places

Northwyke
BHPDG01-759A
1-800-388-7580

3 Bedroom, 2 1/2 Bath

First Floor............. <u>2084 sq ft</u>
Total Living.......... 2084 sq ft
Bonus................... 339 sq ft
Opt. Basement..... 2117 sq ft
Width.................. 62'2"
Depth.................. 49'0"
Foundation.......... Basement or
                     Crawl Space

PLAN PRICE SCHEDULE		
	Crawl	Basement
1 Set	$615	$865
4 Set	$665	$915
8 Set	$725	$975
Vellum	$925	$1,175

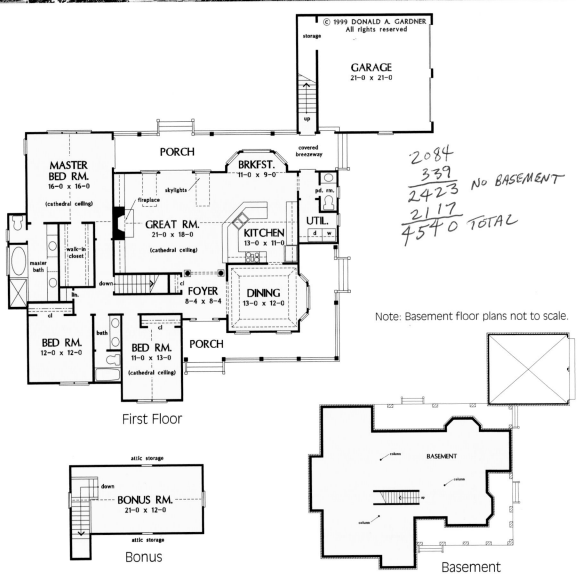

First Floor

```
2084
 339
————  NO BASEMENT
2423
2117
————
4540  TOTAL
```

Note: Basement floor plans not to scale.

BONUS RM.
21-0 x 12-0

Bonus

BASEMENT

Rear Elevation

Basement Tip

Answer the phone with your company's name or formal manner, to not confuse potential clients or colleagues.

Photographed home may have been modified from the original construction documents.

Note: Basement floor plans not to scale.

DECK
23-0 x 10-0
railing

BRKFST.
10-4 x 9-2
pantry

MASTER BED RM.
13-0 x 16-0

GREAT RM.
19-7 x 20-0
(13-0 ceiling)
fireplace
shelves

KIT.
12-7 x 12-4

BED RM.
14-0 x 12-6

bath
walk-in closet

master bath
lin.
cl
lin.

FOYER
5-10 x 12-10
(10-6 ceiling)

bath

DINING
11-4 x 12-10
(12-6 ceiling)

cl
d
w
up
dn.
storage

walk-in closet

BED RM./ STUDY
11-4 x 12-4
(vaulted ceiling)

PORCH

GARAGE
21-4 x 21-0

First Floor

© 2001 DONALD A. GARDNER
All rights reserved

Longleaf
BHPDG01-802A
1-800-388-7580

3 Bedroom, 3 Bath

First Floor............ <u>1995 sq ft</u>
Total Living.......... 1995 sq ft
Bonus.................. 382 sq ft
Opt. Basement..... 2087 sq ft
Width.................. 62'6"
Depth.................. 58'10"
Foundation.......... Basement or Crawl Space

PLAN PRICE SCHEDULE		
	Crawl	Basement
1 Set	$570	$795
4 Set	$620	$845
8 Set	$680	$905
Vellum	$860	$1,085

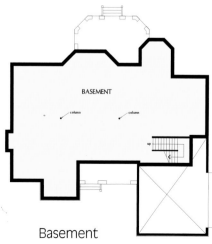

BASEMENT
column
column
up

Basement

BONUS RM.
13-4 x 18-10

7-10 x 4-2
down
attic storage
attic storage

Bonus

Rear Elevation

Business Places

© 2001 Donald A. Gardner, Inc.

Wicklow
BHPDG01-950A
1-800-388-7580

3 Bedroom, 2 1/2 Bath

First Floor.............	1577 sq ft
2nd floor.............	752 sq ft
Total Living..........	2329 sq ft
Bonus..................	470 sq ft
Opt. Basement.....	1661 sq ft
Width..................	44'4"
Depth..................	61'4"
Foundation..........	Basement or Crawl Space

PLAN PRICE SCHEDULE		
	Crawl	Basement
1 Set	$615	$865
4 Set	$665	$915
8 Set	$725	$975
Vellum	$925	$1,175

Rear Elevation

First Floor

Second Floor

Basement

Note: Basement floor plans not to scale.

www.basementhomeplans.com

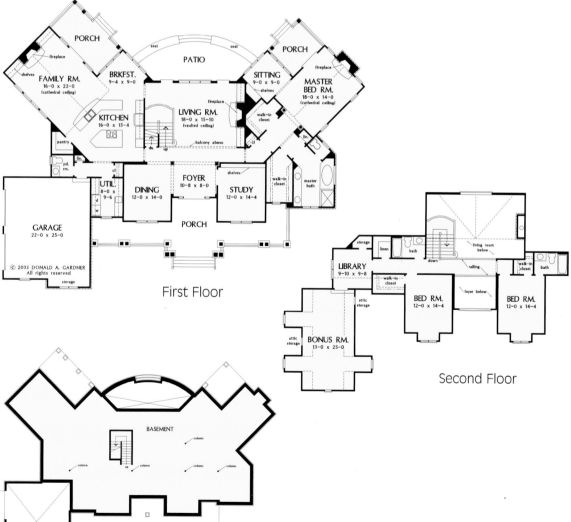

First Floor

Basement

Note: Basement floor plans not to scale.

© 2003 Donald A. Gardner, Inc.

Jerivale
BHPDG01-1033A
1-800-388-7580

3 Bedroom, 3 1/2 Bath

First Floor............	2766 sq ft
2nd floor.............	881 sq ft
Total Living..........	3647 sq ft
Bonus.................	407 sq ft
Opt. Basement.....	2780 sq ft
Width...................	92'5"
Depth...................	71'10"
Foundation..........	Basement or Crawl Space

Second Floor

PLAN PRICE SCHEDULE		
	Crawl	Basement
1 Set	$775	$1,050
4 Set	$825	$1,100
8 Set	$885	$1,160
Vellum	$1,135	$1,410

Rear Elevation

Business Places

Vandenberg
BHPDG01-746D
1-800-388-7580

4 Bedroom, 3 Bath

First Floor............. 1810 sq ft
Basement.............. 1146 sq ft
Total Living........... 2956 sq ft
Width................... 68'4"
Depth.................. 60'10"
Foundation.......... Hillside
Walkout

PLAN PRICE SCHEDULE	
	Walkout
1 Set	$660
4 Set	$710
8 Set	$770
Vellum	$990

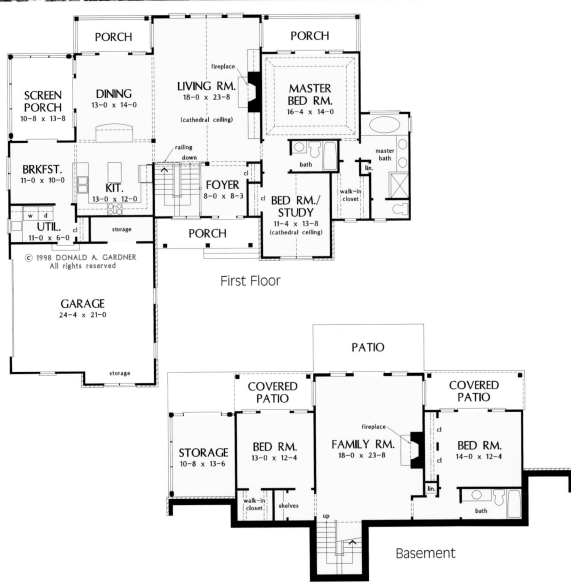

PORCH

SCREEN PORCH
10-8 x 13-8

DINING
13-0 x 14-0

LIVING RM.
18-0 x 23-8

(cathedral ceiling)

fireplace

PORCH

MASTER BED RM.
16-4 x 14-0

master bath

bath

railing down

BRKFST.
11-0 x 10-0

KIT.
13-0 x 12-0

FOYER
8-0 x 8-3

BED RM./STUDY
11-4 x 13-8

(cathedral ceiling)

walk-in closet

lin.

w d

UTIL.
11-0 x 6-0

storage

PORCH

GARAGE
24-4 x 21-0

storage

First Floor

PATIO

COVERED PATIO

COVERED PATIO

STORAGE
10-8 x 13-6

BED RM.
13-0 x 12-4

FAMILY RM.
18-0 x 23-8

fireplace

BED RM.
14-0 x 12-4

walk-in closet

shelves

lin.

up

bath

Basement

Rear Elevation

Business Places

© 2003 Donald A. Gardner, Inc.

Iverson
BHPDG01-1023A
1-800-388-7580

3 Bedroom, 2 Bath

First Floor	1560 sq ft
Total Living	1560 sq ft
Bonus	433 sq ft
Opt. Basement	1618 sq ft
Width	51'8"
Depth	62'0"
Foundation	Basement or Crawl Space

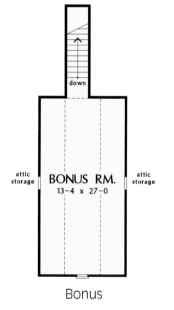

Bonus

attic storage   BONUS RM. 13-4 x 27-0   attic storage

down

Note: Basement floor plans not to scale.

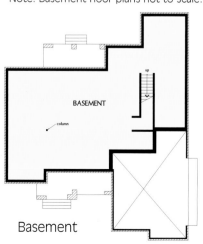

BASEMENT

column

up

Basement

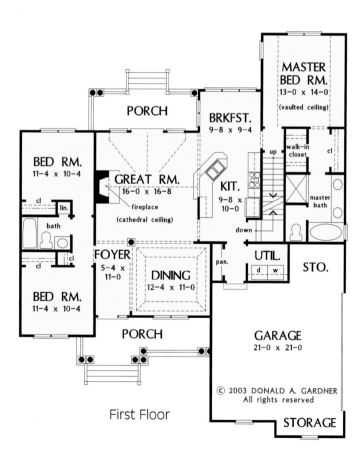

First Floor

PORCH

BED RM. 11-4 x 10-4

GREAT RM. 16-0 x 16-8
fireplace
(cathedral ceiling)

BRKFST. 9-8 x 9-4

KIT. 9-8 x 10-0

MASTER BED RM. 13-0 x 14-0
(vaulted ceiling)

walk-in closet

up

master bath

down

FOYER 5-4 x 11-0

DINING 12-4 x 11-0

bath

BED RM. 11-4 x 10-4

UTIL.
d w

STO.

pan.

PORCH

GARAGE 21-0 x 21-0

STORAGE

PLAN PRICE SCHEDULE

	Crawl	Basement
1 Set	$570	$795
4 Set	$620	$845
8 Set	$680	$905
Vellum	$860	$1,085

Rear Elevation

Business Places

Pennyhill
BHPDG01-294A
1-800-388-7580

3 Bedroom, 2 1/2 Bath

First Floor............. <u>1893 sq ft</u>
Total Living........... 1893 sq ft
Bonus.................. 485 sq ft
Opt. Basement..... 1991 sq ft
Width.................. 71'0"
Depth.................. 56'4"
Foundation.......... Basement or Crawl Space

PLAN PRICE SCHEDULE		
	Crawl	Basement
1 Set	$570	$795
4 Set	$620	$845
8 Set	$680	$905
Vellum	$860	$1,085

First Floor

seat
spa
DECK
PORCH
arched window above door
(cathedral ceiling)
MASTER BED RM.
14-0 x 17-4
master bath
skylights
lin.
walk-in closet
BRKFST.
11-4 x 8-0
up
down
storage
BED RM.
11-4 x 11-0
(cathedral ceiling)
fireplace
KIT.
11-4 x 12-9
d w
UTIL.
GARAGE
23-4 x 23-4
GREAT RM.
15-4 x 18-8
bath
cl
lin.
pd. rm.

BED RM.
13-8 x 11-8
FOYER
7-4 x 11-8
DINING
14-8 x 11-8
PORCH

Note: Basement floor plans not to scale.

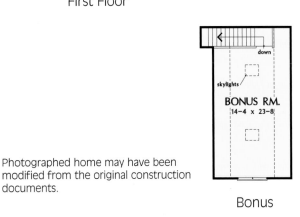

Photographed home may have been modified from the original construction documents.

Rear Elevation

BONUS RM.
14-4 x 23-8
down
skylights

Bonus

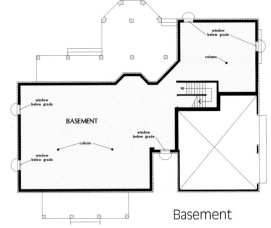

window below grade
column
up
BASEMENT
window below grade
window below grade
column
window below grade

Basement

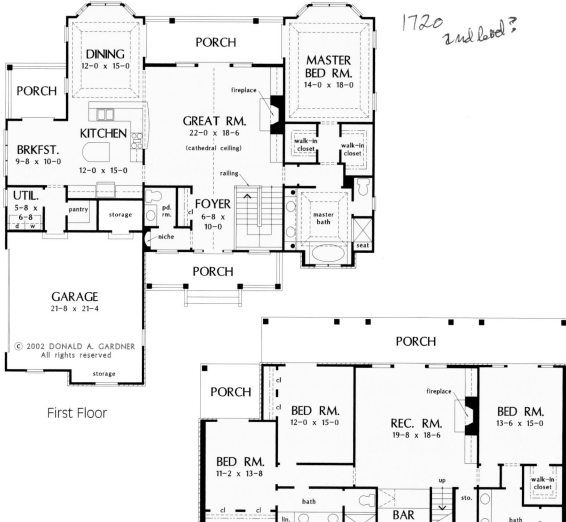

1720 2nd level?

© 2002 Donald A. Gardner, Inc.

Laycrest
BHPDG01-995D
1-800-388-7580

4 Bedroom, 3 1/2 Bath

First Floor............	1720 sq ft
Basement.............	1600 sq ft
Total Living...........	3320 sq ft
Width...................	59'0"
Depth..................	59'4"
Foundation.........	Hillside Walkout

First Floor — DINING 12-0 x 15-0, PORCH, MASTER BED RM. 14-0 x 18-0, fireplace, PORCH, walk-in closet, walk-in closet, GREAT RM. 22-0 x 18-6 (cathedral ceiling), KITCHEN, BRKFST. 9-8 x 10-0, 12-0 x 15-0, railing, UTIL. 5-8 x 6-8, pantry, storage, pd. rm., FOYER 6-8 x 10-0, master bath, niche, seat, GARAGE 21-8 x 21-4, storage, PORCH

Basement — PORCH, BED RM. 12-0 x 15-0, REC. RM. 19-8 x 18-6, fireplace, BED RM. 13-6 x 15-0, BED RM. 11-2 x 13-8, bath, BAR 8-4 x 9-0, wet bar, up, sto., walk-in closet, bath, seat, lin.

PLAN PRICE SCHEDULE	
	Walkout
1 Set	$705
4 Set	$755
8 Set	$815
Vellum	$1055

Rear Elevation

Donald A. Gardner Architects

© 1993 Donald A. Gardner Architects, Inc.

Photographed home may have been modified from the original construction documents.

Irwin
BHPDG01-297A
1-800-388-7580

4 Bedroom, 3 Bath

First Floor............. 1753 sq ft
2nd floor.............. 450 sq ft
Total Living.......... 2203 sq ft
Bonus.................. 376 sq ft
Opt. Basement..... 1715 sq ft
Width................... 55'4"
Depth................... 53'8"
Foundation.......... Basement or Crawl Space

PLAN PRICE SCHEDULE

	Crawl	Basement
1 Set	$615	$865
4 Set	$665	$915
8 Set	$725	$975
Vellum	$925	$1,175

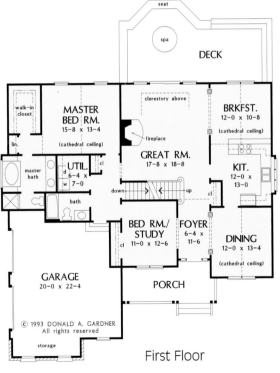

First Floor

MASTER BED RM. 15-8 x 13-4 (cathedral ceiling)
UTIL. 6-4 x 7-0
GREAT RM. 17-8 x 18-8
BRKFST. 12-0 x 10-8 (cathedral ceiling)
KIT. 12-0 x 13-0
BED RM./ STUDY 11-0 x 12-6
FOYER 6-4 x 11-6
DINING 12-0 x 13-4 (cathedral ceiling)
GARAGE 20-0 x 22-4
PORCH
DECK
spa
seat
walk-in closet
master bath
fireplace
cleerstory above
clerestory above
storage

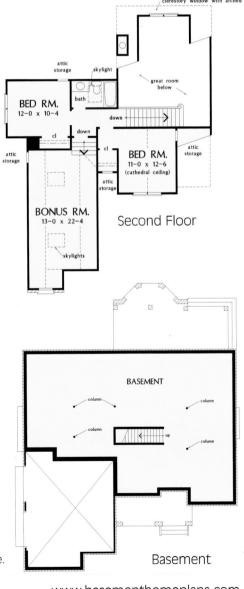

Second Floor

BED RM. 12-0 x 10-4
BED RM. 11-0 x 12-6 (cathedral ceiling)
BONUS RM. 13-0 x 22-4
clerestory window with arched top
attic storage
skylight
bath
great room below
attic storage
skylights

BASEMENT
column

Note: Basement floor plans not to scale.

Basement

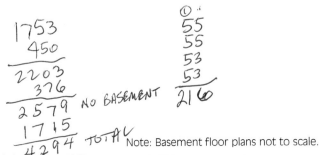

Rear Elevation

www.basementhomeplans.com

Donald A. Gardner Architect

Photographed home may have been modified from the original construction documents.

© 1996 Donald A. Gardner Architects, Inc.

First Floor

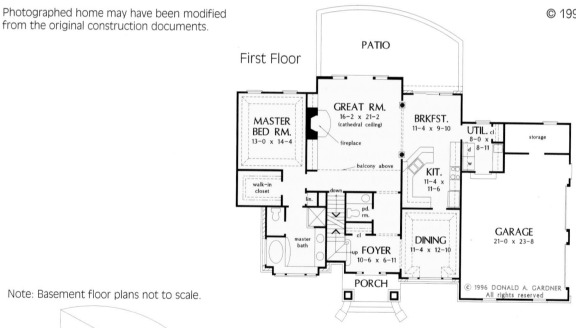

PATIO

GREAT RM.
16-2 x 21-2
(cathedral ceiling)
fireplace

BRKFST.
11-4 x 9-10

UTIL. cl
8-0 x
8-11

storage

MASTER BED RM.
13-0 x 14-4

balcony above

KIT.
11-4 x 11-6

walk-in closet

down

GARAGE
21-0 x 23-8

master bath

lin.

pd. rm.

cl

DINING
11-4 x 12-10

up **FOYER**
10-6 x 6-11

© 1996 DONALD A. GARDNER
All rights reserved

PORCH

Gasden
BHPDG01-431A
1-800-388-7580

3 Bedroom, 2 1/2 Bath

First Floor............. 1585 sq ft
2nd floor............. 617 sq ft
Total Living.......... 2202 sq ft
Bonus................. 353 sq ft
Opt. Basement..... 1586 sq ft
Width.................. 65'8"
Depth.................. 42'6"
Foundation......... Basement or Crawl Space

Note: Basement floor plans not to scale.

PLAN PRICE SCHEDULE		
	Crawl	Basement
1 Set	$615	$865
4 Set	$665	$915
8 Set	$725	$975
Vellum	$925	$1,175

BASEMENT

column

column

up

Basement

great room below

BED RM.
11-4 x 13-8

railing

attic storage

cl

attic storage

down

down

lin.

attic storage

cl

skylights

bath

BONUS RM.
12-0 x 27-4

foyer below

BED RM.
11-4 x 13-10

Second Floor

Rear Elevation

Business Places

© 1996 Donald A. Gardner Architects, Inc.

Rousseau
BHPDG01-451A
1-800-388-7580

3 Bedroom, 2 1/2 Bath

First Floor............ 1904 sq ft
2nd floor............. 645 sq ft
Total Living.......... 2549 sq ft
Bonus.................. 434 sq ft
Opt. Basement..... 1941 sq ft
Width.................. 71'2"
Depth.................. 45'8"
Foundation.......... Basement or Crawl Space

PLAN PRICE SCHEDULE		
	Crawl	Basement
1 Set	$660	$910
4 Set	$710	$960
8 Set	$770	$1,020
Vellum	$990	$1,240

(handwritten notes):
71
45
45
71
232 linear feet

(handwritten notes):
2549
434
2983 No Basement
1941
4924 TOTAL

First Floor

Handwritten within plan area:

PATIO

FAMILY RM. 18-2 x 20-10 (cathedral ceiling) — fireplace — balcony above

MASTER BED RM. 14-0 x 16-0 — walk-in closet — master bath — walk-in closet — lin.

BRKFST. 12-0 x 9-4

UTIL. 8-8 x 8-0 — storage

KIT. 12-0 x 13-0

LIVING RM./STUDY 12-0 x 13-4

pd. rm.

FOYER 11-0 x 8-4

DINING 12-0 x 14-4

GARAGE 21-0 x 24-0

PORCH

down

© 1996 DONALD A. GARDNER
All rights reserved

Basement Tip

Purchase a bookkeeping book, even for the smallest expenses. It can possibly help on future tax breaks for home businesses.

Photographed home may have been modified from the original construction documents.

Note: Basement floor plans not to scale.

Rear Elevation

LOFT/STUDY 9-0 x 14-1 — family room below — railing

BED RM. 13-4 x 11-10

attic storage

skylights

BONUS RM. 21-8 x 16-5

BED RM. 13-4 x 12-2 — walk-in closet — bath — railing — balcony

BED RM. 13-4 x 13-6 — walk-in closet — bath

shelves — down

Second Floor

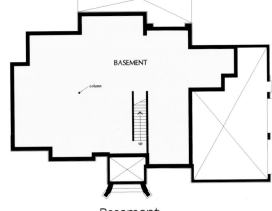

BASEMENT — column

Basement

www.basementhomeplans.com

Business Places

attic storage

down

attic storage

BONUS
11-10 x 24-8

Bonus

PORCH

niche

BRKFST.
11-4 x 12-4

MASTER
BED RM.
13-8 x 15-4

fireplace

GREAT RM.
16-4 x 17-4
(cathedral ceiling)

KITCHEN
13-4 x 12-4

shelves

walk-in closet

linen

master bath

seat

cl

FOYER
13-6 x 6-0

DINING
13-8 x 12-0

PORCH

BED RM.
11-4 x 12-0

bath

cl

lin.

BED RM.
11-4 x 12-0

bath

cl

up

util.

w
d

down

BED RM./
STUDY
11-4 x 12-0

storage

GARAGE
21-4 x 21-0

© 2001 DONALD A. GARDNER
All rights reserved

storage

First Floor

Note: Basement floor plans not to scale.

BASEMENT

column

column

up

Basement

© 2001 Donald A. Gardner, Inc.

Xavier
BHPDG01-960A
1-800-388-7580

4 Bedroom, 3 Bath

First Floor............	**2187 sq ft**
Total Living..........	2187 sq ft
Bonus..................	344 sq ft
Opt. Basement.....	2271 sq ft
Width..................	66'8"
Depth..................	60'2"
Foundation..........	Basement or Crawl Space

PLAN PRICE SCHEDULE		
	Crawl	Basement
1 Set	$615	$865
4 Set	$665	$915
8 Set	$725	$975
Vellum	$925	$1,175

Rear Elevation

Donald A. Gardner Architects

© 2002 Donald A. Gardner, Inc.

Gentry
BHPDG01-977A
1-800-388-7580

3 Bedroom, 2 Bath

First Floor	1882 sq ft
Total Living	1882 sq ft
Bonus	424 sq ft
Opt. Basement	1961 sq ft
Width	61'8"
Depth	66'4"
Foundation	Basement or Crawl Space

PLAN PRICE SCHEDULE

	Crawl	Basement
1 Set	$570	$795
4 Set	$620	$845
8 Set	$680	$905
Vellum	$860	$1,085

First Floor

DECK
18-8 x 8-0

GREAT RM.
18-0 x 17-4
(cathedral ceiling)
fireplace
shelves

MASTER BED RM.
13-0 x 17-4

KITCHEN
13-0 x 10-0

BRKFST.
9-0 x 10-0

PORCH

BED RM.
12-0 x 11-0

FOYER
6-0 x 12-8

DINING
13-0 x 12-8

bath

UTILITY
6-0 x 12-8

BED RM.
12-0 x 11-0

walk-in closet

master bath

lin.

PORCH

walk-in closet

storage

GARAGE
22-0 x 21-8

sto.

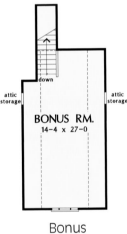

BONUS RM.
14-4 x 27-0

attic storage   attic storage

down

Bonus

Note: Basement floor plans not to scale.

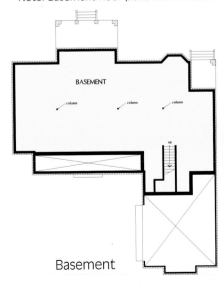

BASEMENT

column   column   column

up

Basement

Rear Elevation

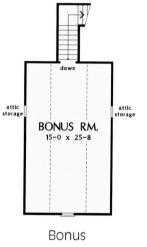

Bonus

BONUS RM.
15-0 x 25-8

attic storage

attic storage

down

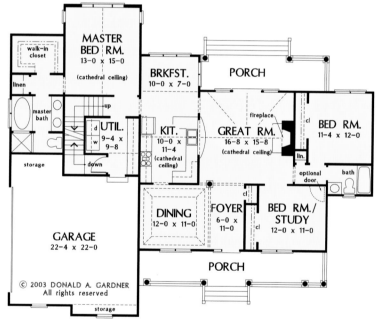

First Floor

walk-in closet

MASTER BED RM.
13-0 x 15-0
(cathedral ceiling)

linen

master bath

UTIL.
9-4 x 9-8

storage

GARAGE
22-4 x 22-0

BRKFST.
10-0 x 7-0

KIT.
10-0 x 11-4
(cathedral ceiling)

PORCH

GREAT RM.
16-8 x 15-8
(cathedral ceiling)

fireplace

BED RM.
11-4 x 12-0

DINING
12-0 x 11-0

FOYER
6-0 x 11-0

BED RM./ STUDY
12-0 x 11-0

optional door

bath

PORCH

storage

© 2003 Donald A. Gardner, Inc.

Knoxville
BHPDG01-1035A
1-800-388-7580

3 Bedroom, 2 Bath

First Floor............. 1700 sq ft
Total Living........... 1700 sq ft
Bonus.................. 413 sq ft
Opt. Basement...... 1744 sq ft
Width.................... 64'4"
Depth....................53'6"
Foundation...........Basement or Crawl Space

PLAN PRICE SCHEDULE		
	Crawl	Basement
1 Set	$570	$795
4 Set	$620	$845
8 Set	$680	$905
Vellum	$860	$1,085

Note: Basement floor plans not to scale.

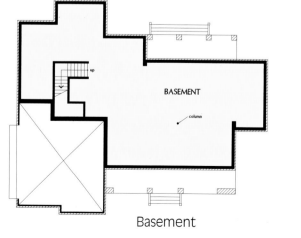

Basement

BASEMENT

up

column

1700
413
2113 NO BASEMENT
1744
3857 TOTAL

① 64
64
53
53
234 linear

Rear Elevation

Donald A. Gardner Architects

© 2004 Donald A. Gardner, Inc.

East Haven
BHPDG01-1049A
1-800-388-7580

4 Bedroom, 3 Bath

First Floor............. 2710 sq ft
Total Living........... 2710 sq ft
Bonus................... 454 sq ft
Opt. Basement...... 2790 sq ft
Width................... 69'8"
Depth.................. 72'10"
Foundation.......... Basement or Crawl Space

PLAN PRICE SCHEDULE		
	Crawl	Basement
1 Set	$660	$910
4 Set	$710	$960
8 Set	$770	$1,020
Vellum	$990	$1,240

First Floor

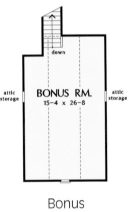

Bonus

Note: Basement floor plans not to scale.

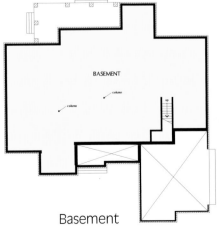

Basement

Rear Elevation

www.basementhomeplans.com

Business Places

Basement Tip

Take advantage of the large space by building walls to create multiple rooms.

First Floor

PORCH

BRKFST.
12-0 x 13-0

BED RM.
12-0 x 12-0

fireplace

GREAT RM.
16-4 x 19-8
(cathedral ceiling)

KIT.
12-0 x 12-0

walk-in closet

MASTER BED RM.
14-0 x 16-0

cl
lin.
bath

pd. rm.

BED RM./ STUDY
14-0 x 12-0

cl

FOYER
7-8 x 12-4

DINING
14-4 x 12-0

cl
cl

UTIL.
8-4 x 12-0

up

master bath

w
d

seat

down

storage

PORCH

GARAGE
22-4 x 21-0

storage

© 2002 Donald A. Gardner, Inc.

Fernley
BHPDG01-980A
1-800-388-7580

3 Bedroom, 2 1/2 Bath

First Floor.............	2055 sq ft
Total Living...........	2055 sq ft
Bonus..................	400 sq ft
Opt. Basement......	2119 sq ft
Width....................	62'4"
Depth....................	65'4"
Foundation...........	Basement or Crawl Space

PLAN PRICE SCHEDULE		
	Crawl	Basement
1 Set	$615	$865
4 Set	$665	$915
8 Set	$725	$975
Vellum	$925	$1,175

Note: Basement floor plans not to scale.

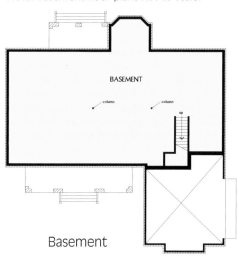

BASEMENT

column   column

up

Basement

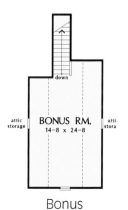

down

attic storage

BONUS RM.
14-8 x 24-8

attic storage

Bonus

Rear Elevation

Donald A. Gardner Architects

© 1999 Donald A. Gardner, Inc.

Loxdale
BHPDG01-788D
1-800-388-7580

4 Bedroom, 3 1/2 Bath

First Floor	1734 sq ft
Second Floor	546 sq ft
Basement	788 sq ft
Total Living	3068 sq ft
Bonus	381 sq ft
Width	60'8"
Depth	68'0"
Foundation	Hillside Walkout

PLAN PRICE SCHEDULE

	Walkout
1 Set	$705
4 Set	$755
8 Set	$815
Vellum	$1,055

Rear Elevation

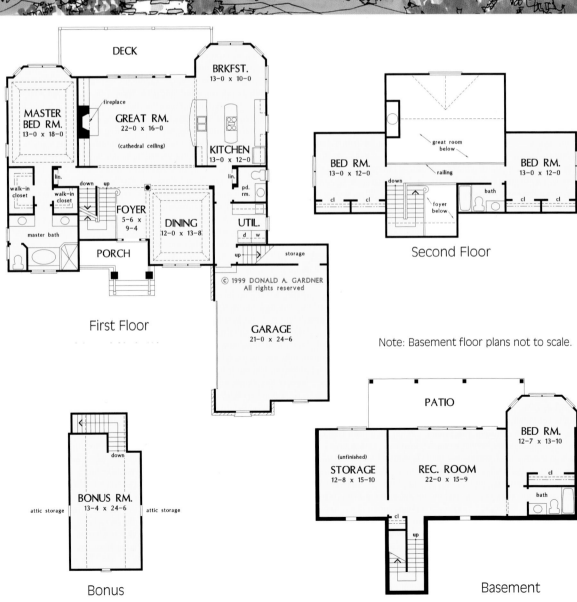

First Floor

- DECK
- BRKFST. 13-0 x 10-0
- fireplace
- MASTER BED RM. 13-0 x 18-0
- GREAT RM. 22-0 x 16-0 (cathedral ceiling)
- KITCHEN 13-0 x 12-0
- walk-in closet
- walk-in closet
- lin.
- down / up
- FOYER 5-6 x 9-4
- DINING 12-0 x 13-8
- pd. rm.
- UTIL.
- master bath
- PORCH
- up
- storage
- © 1999 DONALD A. GARDNER All rights reserved
- GARAGE 21-0 x 24-6

Second Floor

- BED RM. 13-0 x 12-0
- great room below
- railing
- down
- foyer below
- bath
- BED RM. 13-0 x 12-0

Note: Basement floor plans not to scale.

Bonus

- down
- BONUS RM. 13-4 x 24-6
- attic storage
- attic storage

Basement

- PATIO
- BED RM. 12-7 x 13-10
- STORAGE 12-8 x 15-10 (unfinished)
- REC. ROOM 22-0 x 15-9
- bath
- up

© 2000 Donald A. Gardner, Inc.

Steeplechase
BHPDG01-876D
1-800-388-7580

5 Bedroom, 4 Bath, 2 Half Baths

First Floor	3040 sq ft
Basement	1736 sq ft
Total Living	4776 sq ft
Width	106'1"
Depth	104'2"
Foundation	Hillside Walkout

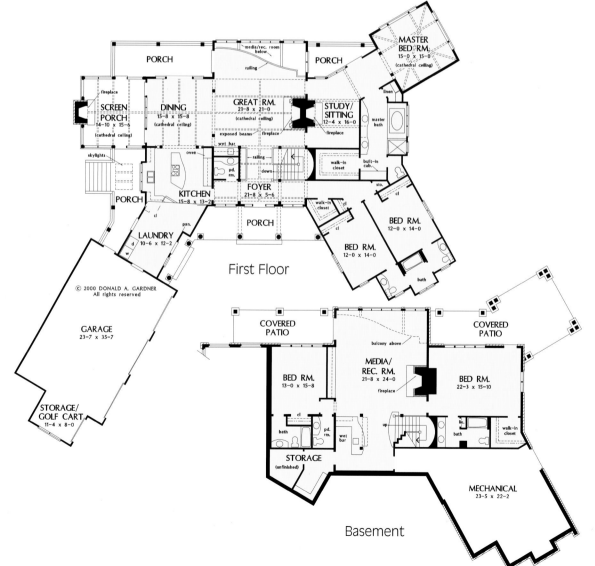

First Floor

Basement

PLAN PRICE SCHEDULE

	Walkout
1 Set	$950
4 Set	$1,000
8 Set	$1,060
Vellum	$1,315

Rear Elevation

Donald A. Gardner Architects

© 2002 Donald A. Gardner, Inc.

Gillespie
BHPDG01-992A
1-800-388-7580

3 Bedroom, 2 Bath

First Floor.............	<u>1970 sq ft</u>
Total Living...........	1970 sq ft
Bonus..................	369 sq ft
Opt. Basement......	2022 sq ft
Width..................	56'0"
Depth..................	62'0"
Foundation..........	Basement or Crawl Space

PLAN PRICE SCHEDULE

	Crawl	Basement
1 Set	$570	$795
4 Set	$620	$845
8 Set	$680	$905
Vellum	$860	$1,085

First Floor

© 2002 DONALD A. GARDNER
All rights reserved

PORCH

BRKFST.
11-4 x 10-4

MASTER BED RM.
13-8 x 16-0

fireplace

GREAT RM.
17-0 x 20-0

KIT.
11-4 x 12-0

walk-in closet

walk-in closet

BED RM.
12-0 x 12-0

cl

FOYER
6-0 x 13-0

DINING
12-8 x 13-0

UTIL.
6-4 x 8-10

up

master bath

lin.

BED RM.
12-0 x 12-0

cl

PORCH

dn.

STORAGE

GARAGE
21-0 x 21-0

bath

Basement Tip

Install plenty of recessed fixtures in the basement to ensure bright and evenly distributed light.

Note: Basement floor plans not to scale.

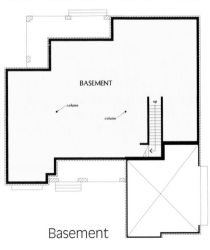

BASEMENT

column

column

up

Basement

BONUS RM.
13-4 x 24-8

attic storage

attic storage

down

Bonus

Rear Elevation

www.basementhomeplans.com

Donald A. Gardner Architect

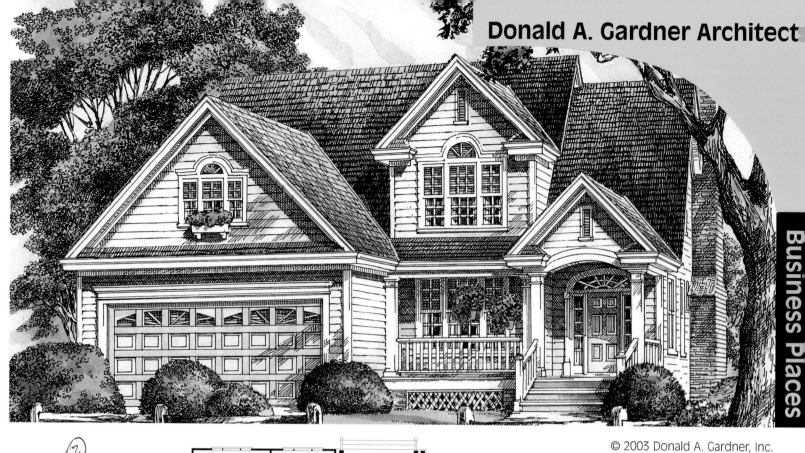

First Floor

MASTER BED RM. 14-8 x 14-0 (vaulted ceiling)

BRKFST. 12-0 x 11-8

PORCH

walk-in closet

cl

KIT. 12-0 x 10-8

GREAT RM. 16-10 x 18-0 (vaulted ceiling)

fireplace

master bath

lin.

UTIL. 5-10 x 5-8

pd. rm.

dn.

up

w d

cl

FOYER 7-6 x 9-8 (vaulted ceiling)

DINING 11-8 x 13-8

GARAGE 22-0 x 22-0

PORCH

Handwritten notes:
(2)
47
47
55
55
204 linear

1569
504
2073
320
2393 N.O BASEMENT
1569
3962 TOTAL

Dayton
BHPDG01-1008A
1-800-388-7580

3 Bedroom, 2 1/2 Bath

First Floor.............	1569 sq ft
Second Floor........	504 sq ft
Total Living...........	2073 sq ft
Bonus...................	320 sq ft
Opt. Basement......	1569 sq ft
Width....................	47'0"
Depth....................	55'0"
Foundation............	Basement or Crawl Space

PLAN PRICE SCHEDULE		
	Crawl	Basement
1 Set	$615	$865
4 Set	$665	$915
8 Set	$725	$975
Vellum	$925	$1,175

Note: Basement floor plans not to scale.

column

BASEMENT

up

Basement

attic storage

walk-in closet

bath

shelf

great room below

BED RM. 11-0 x 12-0

down

down

lin.

cl

shelf

foyer below

BED RM. 11-8 x 11-4 (vaulted ceiling)

attic storage

BONUS RM. 13-4 x 22-0 (vaulted ceiling)

attic storage

Second Floor

Rear Elevation

HEALTHY HABITATS

People are more aware of their health today than ever. Workout facilities are on every street corner. While most people are anxious to get in shape, lack of time often hinders them from hitting the gym. Think of how easy it would be to walk downstairs and have a fully functional fitness club in your own home.

Before throwing some free-weights and a treadmill in your basement, consult with your family to determine your fitness needs. What do you want from a home gym? While some might enjoy an open spot for yoga or gymnastics,

...For all your fitness needs

others might need room for weight lifting and cardio equipment. These factors are all important when choosing the equipment, flooring and design of your gym. Establishing your needs will help you better plan for your new facility.

Enhance your gym décor by making it as comfortable as possible. Surrounding yourself with family pictures and memoirs creates a fun, comfortable environment that will help you relax. Installing mirrors assures proper posture when lifting weights or memorizing an aerobic routine. Two mirrors placed at 90 degrees will create an illusion of space and open up a smaller room.

Lighting is also a substantial component for the home gym. Recessed pot lights work well and don't deduct from headroom. A heavily lit room enables proper operation of workout equipment.

Consider installing a kitchenette nearby so sports drinks and quick snacks are readily available. Being close to refreshments is always a bonus after a hard workout.

For those who want the ultimate home gym, the following basement floor plans provide a great spot for installing a sauna, aerobic facility or basic place to tone up. Whatever your fitness needs, the basement is a great private area for getting in shape.

© 2000 Donald A. Gardner, Inc.

COUNTRY CHARMER

Above: An arched transom crowns three windows to enable a sneak peek at Mother Nature when enjoying meals.

Left: The basement level features multiple sets of French doors to provide stimulating scenery when exercising.

Above: Exposed wooden beams and a cathedral ceiling enhance the lofty great room, made more appealing by double doors that promote natural sunlight.

Basement Tip

✔ *Hang bulletin or dry erase boards to track progress with weight loss, burned calories and distances.*

Twin dormers, cedar-shake siding and stone add curb appeal to this Craftsman design. Charming yet refined, the *Adelaide* is a classic combination of a traditional country home and an impressive, spacious floor plan. Exposed wooden beams and a natural-looking exterior bring the countryside one step closer, along with two decks, a screened porch and a spacious patio. From the front-entry garage to the multiple rear porches, the *Adelaide* is continuous convenience intermingled with stylish features.

Above: An expanse of countertops becomes instant gathering spots for snacking and chatting.

Wraparound countertops in the kitchen create an instant partition yet still allow a natural traffic flow between the great and breakfast rooms. Ceiling treatments throughout the floor plan continue the feel of spaciousness.

The large master suite features an adjacent private deck overlooking the back patio, while dual walk-in closets and a large bathroom simplify morning rituals. Located in the rear of the home, the master bedroom provides the utmost privacy.

Architectural detail shines throughout the floor plan. Various ceiling treatments crown several rooms, adding vertical volume to each, and storage space is around every corner. From decorative columns to multiple fireplaces, walk-in closets and a shower seat, niceties are abundant.

The basement level not only features two additional bedrooms and a covered patio, but also a large rec room for a home gym. For the fitness enthusiast, this

Above: The adjacent porch and wall of windows create a scenic breakfast room.

Left: The screened porch elegantly combines outdoor enjoyment with indoor ease.

Left: Built-in shelves and a wet bar make refreshment and convenience one step closer.

room at the base of the stairs assures a short walk to your new workout facility. Double French doors brighten the room and enable a view when working out on a treadmill or stationary bike.

The adjacent storage areas are ideal for storing dumbbells, tennis shoes and workout tapes.

The **Adelaide** provides abundant space for getting fit and leaves the formal, elegant living rooms above.

Below: The cedar-shake exterior and stable-style garage doors exude irresistible curb appeal, while full windows frame the front door for a welcoming entry.

© 1999 Donald A. Gardner, Inc.

Adelaide

BHPDG01-866D

4 Bedroom, 3 Bath
First Floor.........2151 sq ft
Basement.........<u>1150 sq ft</u>
Total Living.......3301 sq ft
Width.............. 83' 0"
Depth.............. 74' 4"
Foundation...... Hillside
Walkout

1-800-388-7580
www.basementhomeplans.com

Please Note: Home photographed may differ from actual construction documents.

PLAN PRICE SCHEDULE	
	Walkout
1 Set	$705
4 Set	$755
8 Set	$815
Vellum	$1,055

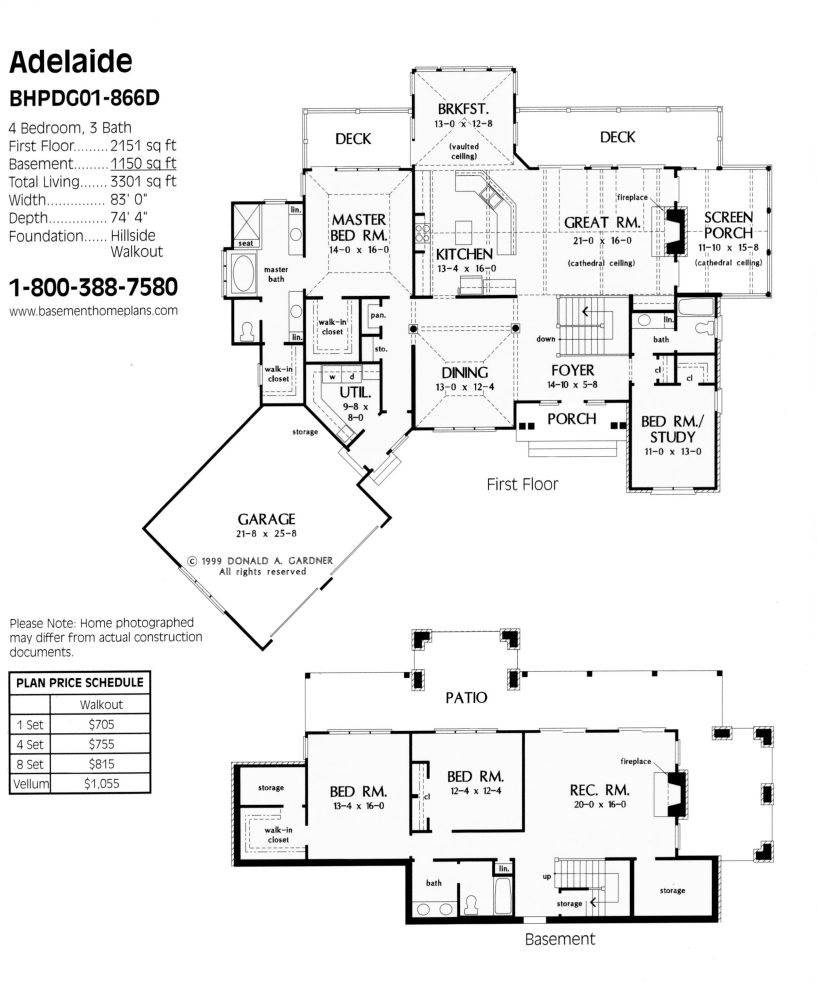

BRKFST.
13-0 x 12-8
(vaulted ceiling)

DECK

DECK

fireplace

GREAT RM.
21-0 x 16-0
(cathedral ceiling)

SCREEN PORCH
11-10 x 15-8
(cathedral ceiling)

MASTER BED RM.
14-0 x 16-0

KITCHEN
13-4 x 16-0

lin.

master bath
seat

walk-in closet

pan.

sto.

walk-in closet

w d

UTIL.
9-8 x 8-0

storage

DINING
13-0 x 12-4

down

bath

lin.

FOYER
14-10 x 5-8

cl

cl

PORCH

BED RM./ STUDY
11-0 x 13-0

GARAGE
21-8 x 25-8

First Floor

PATIO

storage

BED RM.
13-4 x 16-0

walk-in closet

cl

BED RM.
12-4 x 12-4

fireplace

REC. RM.
20-0 x 16-0

bath

lin.

up

storage

storage

storage

Basement

Two-story portico and decorative keystones combine with multiple gables for an alluring exterior.

© 1997 Donald A. Gardner Architects, Inc.

LAVISH LIVING

Ornately detailed, the great room's wall of windows illuminates the entire living area.

Basement Tip

✓ Assemble climbing rocks in fun forms, like words or shapes, to keep kids interested while exercising.

A clerestory window, detailed columns, and French doors lend drama to the **Montpelier's** grand entry. Inside, luxury abounds with a formal living room/study with fireplace and box bay window. Open to the kitchen and breakfast bay, the two-story family room boasts a fireplace flanked by built-in cabinetry.

Above: Dual sinks built into the island yield more counter space for meal preparation.

An office located at the back of the home includes a private bath. This could also act as a secondary master suite.

The master suite features a sitting area to promote a tranquil space, as well as a generous walk-in closet. The upstairs level includes a graceful balcony, two bedrooms with walk-in closets, a full bath and bonus room. The spacious utility room has a convenient built-in counter and large soaking sink perfect for grooming pets.

Encouraging physical activity for children is no longer difficult with the expansive basement level. Perfect for a kid's climbing wall or gymnastics area, the basement leaves plenty of room for cartwheels.

Basement Tip

✓ *Rubber mats or thick, plush carpeting create a soft floor for stretching before climbing.*

Above: Bay windows and a rear deck enhance the lavish brick exterior

Note: Basement floor plans not to scale.

Rear Elevation

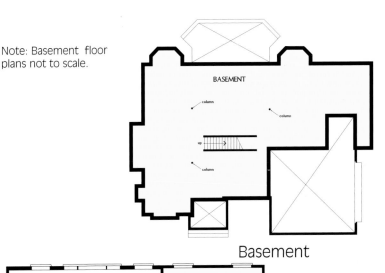

Basement

Montpelier

BHPDG01-483A

4 Bedroom, 3 1/2 Bath

First Floor.......... 2249 sq ft

Second Floor..... 620 sq ft

Total Living......... 2869 sq ft

Bonus................ 308 sq ft

Opt. Basement.. 2255 sq ft

Width................. 69' 6"

Depth................. 52' 0"

Foundation...... Basement or Crawl Space

1-800-388-7580

www.basementhomeplans.com

Please Note: Home photographed may differ from actual construction documents.

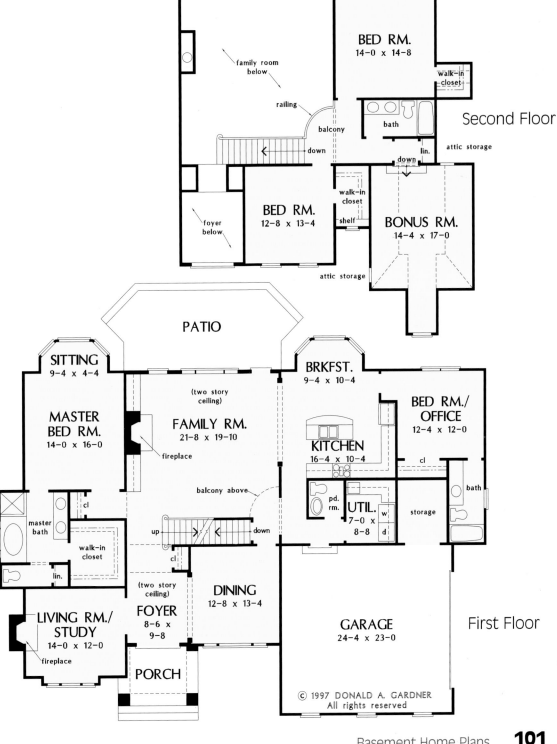

Second Floor

First Floor

© 1997 DONALD A. GARDNER
All rights reserved

© 1998 Donald A. Gardner, Inc.

MOUNTAIN MAJESTIC

Designed for sloping lots, the **Sable Ridge's** stone and stucco exterior takes advantage of rear views, making it a great lakeside or mountain retreat.

The open floor plan features cathedral ceilings in the great room and master bedroom and a tray ceiling in the dining room. A wet bar is conveniently situated between the kitchen and great room, and both the dining and great room access the rear porch.

The master suite maintains privacy on the first floor, and walk-in closets and a well-appointed bath enhance its luxury. Downstairs, two bedrooms share an adjoining bath, and the enormous basement is a perfect area for

Above: The built-in shelves make this large kitchen island a perfect place for cookbooks and stylish decorations.

Left: Dual covered porches create a relaxing way to embrace the outdoors.

setting up a media center or fitness facility.

Ideal for weight-lifting machines and sauna, the basement could be the ultimate room for exercise. The adjacent utility room can function as a place for towels and robes, and the covered patio is great for cooling off after an intense workout.

Below: The stone and stucco façade with covered walkway from the garage give this exterior extra pizzazz.

Sable Ridge
BHPDG01-710D

3 Bedroom, 2 1/2 Bath

First Floor.......... 1472 sq ft

Basement.......... 1211 sq ft

Total Living.........2683 sq ft

Width................ 53' 8"

Depth................ 40' 4"

Foundation...... Hillside Walkout

1-800-388-7580
www.basementhomeplans.com

Please Note: Home photographed may differ from actual construction documents.

PLAN PRICE SCHEDULE	
	Walkout
1 Set	$660
4 Set	$710
8 Set	$770
Vellum	$990

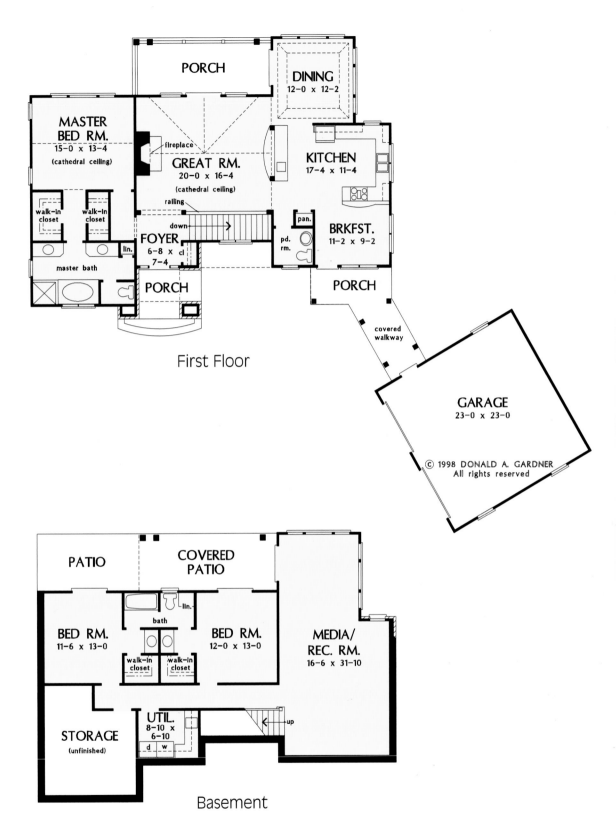

First Floor

Basement

EXTREME STYLE

This updated farmhouse has been given more square footage than a traditional farmhouse and additional custom-styled features. Twin gables, sidelights and an arched entryway accent the façade, while decorative ceiling treatments, bay windows and French doors adorn the interior.

Above: The formal living room/study keeps a natural traffic flow by connecting to a great room and foyer.

Left: This brick farmhouse features arched transoms that echo the barrel-vaulted entry for an impressive exterior.

From an abundance of counter room and large walk-in pantry to the built-ins and storage areas throughout the home, this design makes the most of space. Supported by columns, a curved balcony overlooks the stunning two-story great room. The powder room is easily accessible from the common room, and angled corners soften the dining room.

For those who need wide-open, flexible spaces, the bonus room and basement can add almost 2,400 additional square feet of living or playing area. Create a children's retreat in the bonus area and a workout space in the basement for great family together times.

Rear Elevation

(handwritten notes)
① 71
71
54
54
250 linear feet

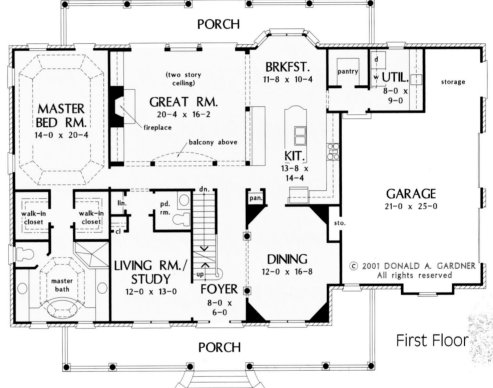

Note: Basement floor plans not to scale.

BASEMENT

column
column

up

Basement

PORCH

(two story ceiling)

BRKFST.
11-8 x 10-4

pantry

UTIL.
8-0 x 9-0

storage

GREAT RM.
20-4 x 16-2

fireplace

balcony above

KIT.
13-8 x 14-4

MASTER
BED RM.
14-0 x 20-4

walk-in closet

walk-in closet

lin.

cl

pd. rm.

dn.

pan.

GARAGE
21-0 x 25-0

sto.

master bath

LIVING RM./
STUDY
12-0 x 13-0

up

FOYER
8-0 x 6-0

DINING
12-0 x 16-8

© 2001 DONALD A. GARDNER
All rights reserved

First Floor

PORCH

Hickory Ridge

BHPDG01-916A

4 Bedroom, 3 1/2 Bath
First Floor............2194 sq ft
Second Floor.......973 sq ft.
Total Living..........3167 sq ft
Bonus..................281 sq ft
Opt. Basement....2194 sq ft
Width..................71' 11"
Depth..................54' 4"
Foundation.........Basement or
Crawl Space

1-800-388-7580
www.basementhomeplans.com

(handwritten calculations)
2194
973
3167
281
3448 NO BASEMENT
2194
5642 TOTAL

Please Note: Home photographed may differ from actual construction documents.

great room below

BED RM.
12-0 x 14-0

attic storage

railing

cl

cl

down

BONUS RM.
14-10 x 17-0

7-0 x 6-0

walk-in closet

bath

down

bath

walk-in closet

attic storage

BED RM.
12-0 x 13-0

foyer below

BED RM.
12-0 x 13-0

Second Floor

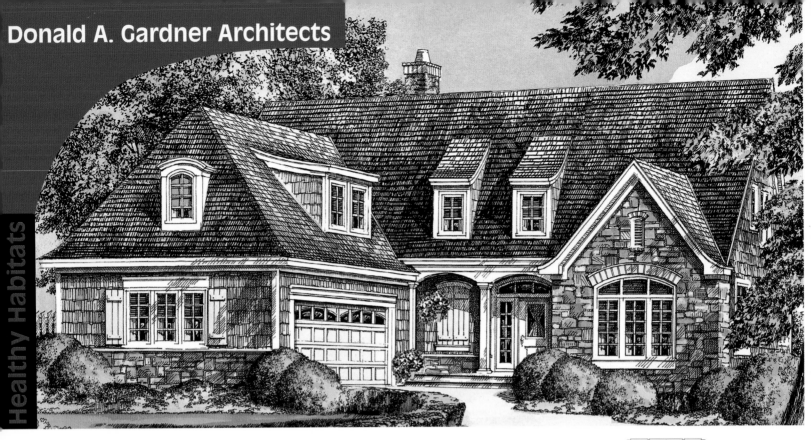

Healthy Habitats

Newcastle
BHPDG01-994A
1-800-388-7580

3 Bedroom, 3 1/2 Bath

First Floor	1834 sq ft
Second Floor	681 sq ft
Total Living	2515 sq ft
Bonus	365 sq ft
Opt. Basement	1825 sq ft
Width	50'8"
Depth	66'8"
Foundation	Basement or Crawl Space

PLAN PRICE SCHEDULE		
	Crawl	Basement
1 Set	$660	$910
4 Set	$710	$960
8 Set	$770	$1,020
Vellum	$990	$1,240

Rear Elevation

First Floor

© 2002 DONALD A. GARDNER
All rights reserved

Second Floor

Note: Basement floor plans not to scale.

Basement

Healthy Habitats

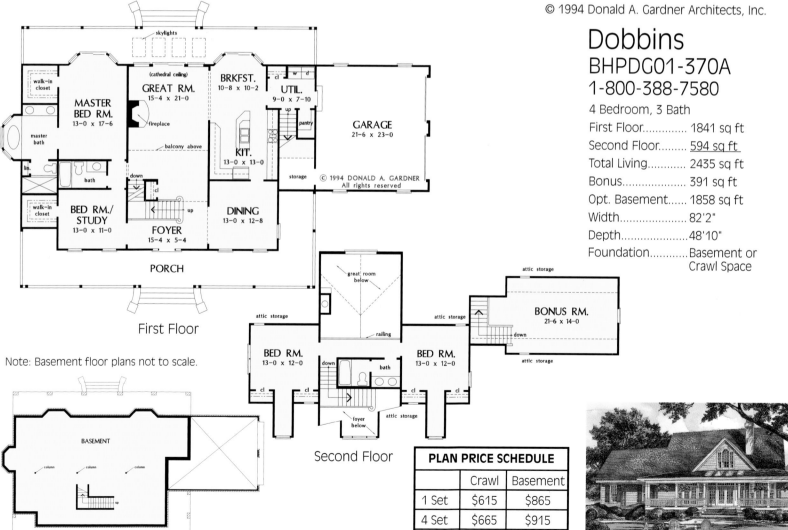

First Floor

skylights

walk-in closet

MASTER BED RM.
13-0 x 17-6

master bath

lin.

bath

walk-in closet

BED RM./ STUDY
13-0 x 11-0

(cathedral ceiling)

GREAT RM.
15-4 x 21-0

fireplace

balcony above

down

cl

FOYER
15-4 x 5-4

BRKFST.
10-8 x 10-2

cl   w   d

UTIL.
9-0 x 7-10

up

pantry

KIT.
13-0 x 13-0

DINING
13-0 x 12-8

GARAGE
21-6 x 23-0

storage

© 1994 DONALD A. GARDNER
All rights reserved

PORCH

Note: Basement floor plans not to scale.

Basement

BASEMENT

column   column   column

up

© 1994 Donald A. Gardner Architects, Inc.

Dobbins

BHPDG01-370A
1-800-388-7580

4 Bedroom, 3 Bath

First Floor............. 1841 sq ft
Second Floor......... <u>594 sq ft</u>
Total Living........... 2435 sq ft
Bonus.................... 391 sq ft
Opt. Basement...... 1858 sq ft
Width.................... 82'2"
Depth.................... 48'10"
Foundation............ Basement or Crawl Space

Second Floor

great room below

attic storage

railing

BED RM.
13-0 x 12-0

cl   cl

down

bath

foyer below

attic storage

BED RM.
13-0 x 12-0

cl   cl

attic storage

attic storage

BONUS RM.
21-6 x 14-0

down

attic storage

PLAN PRICE SCHEDULE

	Crawl	Basement
1 Set	$615	$865
4 Set	$665	$915
8 Set	$725	$975
Vellum	$925	$1,175

Rear Elevation

Healthy Habitats

Barclay
BHPDG01-248A
1-800-388-7580

3 Bedroom, 2 1/2 Bath

First Floor.............	1416 sq ft
Second Floor........	445 sq ft
Total Living...........	1861 sq ft
Bonus....................	284 sq ft
Opt. Basement......	1252 sq ft
Width...................	58'3"
Depth...................	53'5"
Foundation..........	Basement or Crawl Space

PLAN PRICE SCHEDULE

	Crawl	Basement
1 Set	$570	$795
4 Set	$620	$845
8 Set	$680	$905
Vellum	$860	$1,085

Rear Elevation

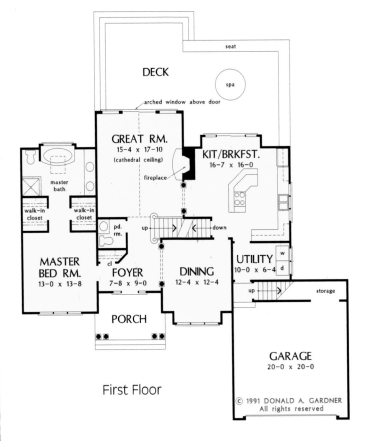

DECK

seat

spa

arched window above door

GREAT RM.
15-4 x 17-10
(cathedral ceiling)

KIT/BRKFST.
16-7 x 16-0

fireplace

master bath

walk-in closet

walk-in closet

pd. rm.

up   down

cl

MASTER BED RM.
13-0 x 13-8

FOYER
7-8 x 9-0

DINING
12-4 x 12-4

UTILITY
10-0 x 6-4

w d

up   storage

PORCH

GARAGE
20-0 x 20-0

First Floor

BED RM.
10-4 x 11-9

attic storage

walk-in closet

down

bath

attic storage

BED RM.
12-4 x 12-0

cl

down

BONUS RM.
11-4 x 23-6

skylights

attic storage

Second Floor

Note: Basement floor plans not to scale.

BASEMENT

window below grade

window below grade

column

column

up

window below grade

window below grade

Basement

Photographed home may have been modified from the original construction documents.

www.basementhomeplans.com

Donald A. Gardner Architects

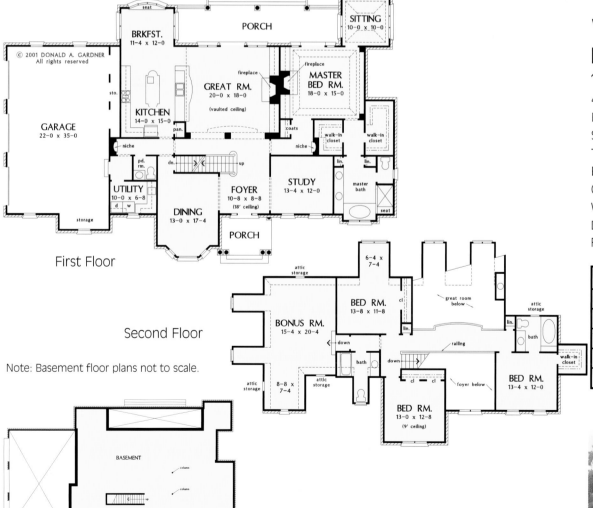

First Floor

Second Floor

Note: Basement floor plans not to scale.

Basement

© 2001 Donald A. Gardner, Inc.

Wellingley
BHPDG01-943A
1-800-388-7580

4 Bedroom, 3 1/2 Bath

First Floor	2511 sq ft
Second Floor	1062 sq ft
Total Living	3573 sq ft
Bonus	465 sq ft
Opt. Basement	2525 sq ft
Width	84'11"
Depth	55'11"
Foundation	Basement or Crawl Space

PLAN PRICE SCHEDULE		
	Crawl	Basement
1 Set	$775	$1,050
4 Set	$825	$1,100
8 Set	$885	$1,160
Vellum	$1,135	$1,410

Rear Elevation

Donald A. Gardner Architects

© 2003 Donald A. Gardner, Inc.

Pinebluff
BHPDG01-1036A
1-800-388-7580

3 Bedroom, 2 Bath

First Floor.............. <u>1634 sq ft</u>
Total Living........... 1634 sq ft
Bonus.................... 425 sq ft
Opt. Basement...... 1734 sq ft
Width.................... 52'11"
Depth.................... 57'4"
Foundation.......... Basement or Crawl Space

PLAN PRICE SCHEDULE		
	Crawl	Basement
1 Set	$570	$795
4 Set	$620	$845
8 Set	$680	$905
Vellum	$860	$1,085

First Floor

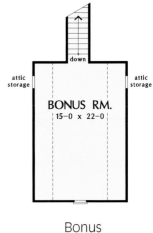

Bonus

Note: Basement floor plans not to scale.

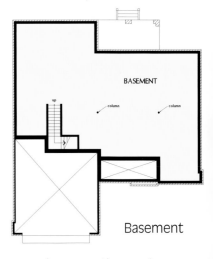

Basement

Rear Elevation

www.basementhomeplans.com

Basement Tip

Position weight-lifting equipment according to the order in which you want to use the machines.

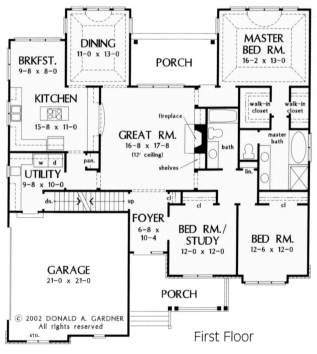

First Floor

© 2002 Donald A. Gardner, Inc.

Wilshire
BHPDG01-976A
1-800-388-7580

3 Bedroom, 2 Bath

First Floor	1929 sq ft
Total Living	1929 sq ft
Bonus	356 sq ft
Opt. Basement	2000 sq ft
Width	53'10"
Depth	57'8"
Foundation	Basement or Crawl Space

PLAN PRICE SCHEDULE		
	Crawl	Basement
1 Set	$570	$795
4 Set	$620	$845
8 Set	$680	$905
Vellum	$860	$1,085

Note: Basement floor plans not to scale.

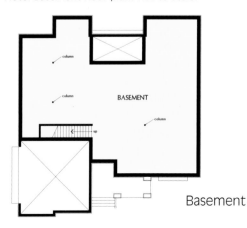

Basement

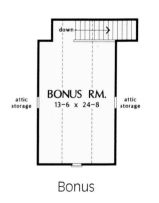

Bonus

Rear Elevation

Healthy Habitats

© 1995 Donald A. Gardner Architects, Inc.

Hampton
BHPDG01-390A
1-800-388-7580

3 Bedroom, 2 Bath

First Floor..............	<u>1857 sq ft</u>
Total Living............	1857 sq ft
Bonus....................	360 sq ft
Opt. Basement......	1920 sq ft
Width....................	66'4"
Depth....................	55'2"
Foundation..........	Basement or Crawl Space

PLAN PRICE SCHEDULE		
	Crawl	Basement
1 Set	$570	$795
4 Set	$620	$845
8 Set	$680	$905
Vellum	$860	$1,085

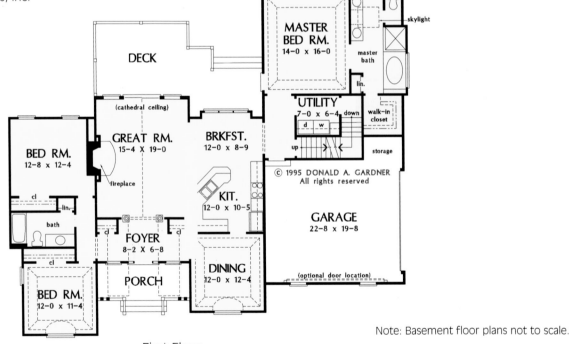

First Floor

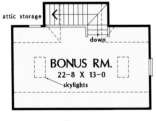

Bonus

Note: Basement floor plans not to scale.

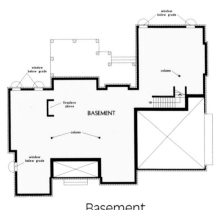

Basement

Rear Elevation

Photographed home may have been modified from the original construction documents.

www.basementhomeplans.com

Healthy Habitats

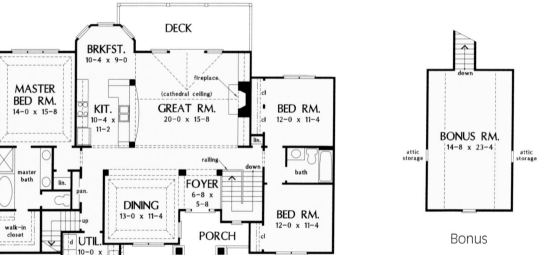

DECK

BRKFST.
10-4 x 9-0

MASTER BED RM.
14-0 x 15-8

fireplace

(cathedral ceiling)

KIT.
10-4 x 11-2

GREAT RM.
20-0 x 15-8

BED RM.
12-0 x 11-4

cl
cl
lin.

master bath

lin.

pan.

railing

down

bath

walk-in closet

FOYER
6-8 x 5-8

down

DINING
13-0 x 11-4

up

BED RM.
12-0 x 11-4

storage

UTIL.
10-0 x 5-6

d
w

PORCH

cl

GARAGE
22-0 x 23-4

© 1999 DONALD A. GARDNER
All rights reserved

First Floor

down

BONUS RM.
14-8 x 23-4

attic storage

attic storage

Bonus

© 1999 Donald A. Gardner, Inc.

Thistlewood
BHPDG01-787D
1-800-388-7580

4 Bedroom, 3 Bath

First Floor............. 1864 sq ft
Basement............. 999 sq ft
Total Living........... 2863 sq ft
Bonus................... 417 sq ft
Width................... 60'0"
Depth................... 67'2"
Foundation........... Hillside Walkout

PLAN PRICE SCHEDULE	
	Walkout
1 Set	$660
4 Set	$710
8 Set	$770
Vellum	$990

PATIO

BED RM.
13-7 x 15-8

REC. ROOM
29-0 x 15-8

(unfinished)
STORAGE
15-4 x 11-5

walk-in closet

bath

lin.

cl

up

Basement

Rear Elevation

Donald A. Gardner Architects

© 2003 Donald A. Gardner, Inc.

Bookworth
BHPDG01-1027A
1-800-388-7580

3 Bedroom, 2 Bath

First Floor............. <u>1854 sq ft</u>
Total Living........... 1854 sq ft
Opt. Basement...... 1911 sq ft
Width.................. 65'6"
Depth.................. 62'6"
Foundation.......... Basement or Crawl Space

PLAN PRICE SCHEDULE		
	Crawl	Basement
1 Set	$570	$795
4 Set	$620	$845
8 Set	$680	$905
Vellum	$860	$1,085

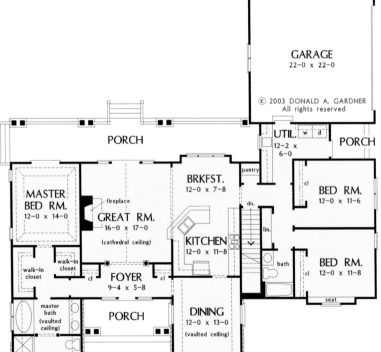

First Floor

Note: Basement floor plans not to scale.

Basement

Rear Elevation

Healthy Habitats

Photographed home may have been modified from the original construction documents.

© 2003 Donald A. Gardner, Inc.

Colridge
BHPDG01-1012D
1-800-388-7580

3 Bedroom, 3 Bath

First Floor............. 1732 sq ft
Basement............. 920 sq ft
Total Living........... 2652 sq ft
Width.................... 70'6"
Depth....................59'6"
Foundation...........Hillside Walkout

First Floor

DINING
12-0 x 12-4

DECK

KIT.
11-2 x 17-4

LIVING RM.
20-10 x 17-4
(cathedral ceiling)

fireplace

SCREEN PORCH
14-0 x 13-8

shelves

pantry

railing

pantry

cl

bath

MASTER BED RM.
14-0 x 15-0
(10'-6" ceiling)

down

UTIL.
9-0 x 9-10

w
d

FOYER
10-0 x 6-2

BED RM./STUDY
13-6 x 11-4

cl

walk-in closet

walk-in closet

GARAGE
22-0 x 22-8

PORCH

seat

storage

master bath

lin.

lin.

PLAN PRICE SCHEDULE	
	Walkout
1 Set	$660
4 Set	$710
8 Set	$770
Vellum	$990

Basement

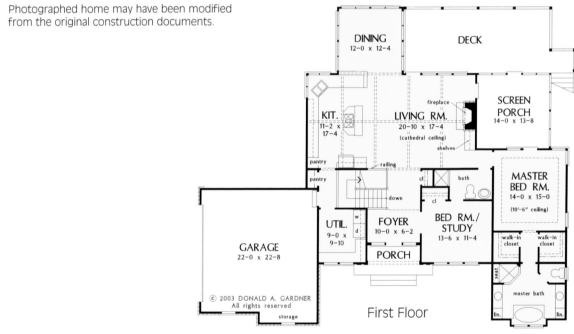

OFFICE
12-0 x 12-0

PATIO

BED RM.
13-2 x 12-0

FAMILY RM.
17-8 x 17-4

walk-in closet

bath

up

STORAGE
(unfinished)

sto.

sto.

Rear Elevation

Healthy Habitats

Irby
BHPDG01-993A
1-800-388-7580

3 Bedroom, 2 Bath

First Floor..............	1580 sq ft
Total Living...........	1580 sq ft
Bonus...................	423 sq ft
Opt. Basement......	1669 sq ft
Width..................	55'6"
Depth..................	49'8"
Foundation..........	Basement or Crawl Space

PLAN PRICE SCHEDULE		
	Crawl	Basement
1 Set	$570	$795
4 Set	$620	$845
8 Set	$680	$905
Vellum	$860	$1,085

First Floor

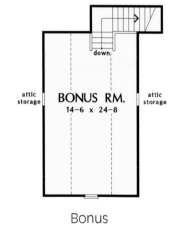

Bonus

Note: Basement floor plans not to scale.

Basement

Rear Elevation

Basement Tip

Be sure to install outlets that are capable of handling your workout equipment's higher voltage needs.

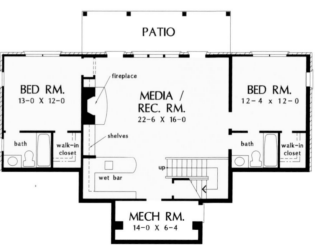

PATIO

BED RM.
13-0 X 12-0

fireplace

MEDIA /
REC. RM.
22-6 X 16-0

BED RM.
12-4 x 12-0

shelves

bath

walk-in closet

bath

walk-in closet

wet bar

up

MECH RM.
14-0 X 6-4

Basement

© 1998 Donald A. Gardner, Inc.

Berkshire
BHPDG01-748D
1-800-388-7580

4 Bedroom, 3 1/2 Bath

First Floor	2065 sq ft
Basement	1216 sq ft
Total Living	3281 sq ft
Width	82'2"
Depth	43'6"
Foundation	Hillside Walkout

PLAN PRICE SCHEDULE	
	Walkout
1 Set	$705
4 Set	$755
8 Set	$815
Vellum	$1,055

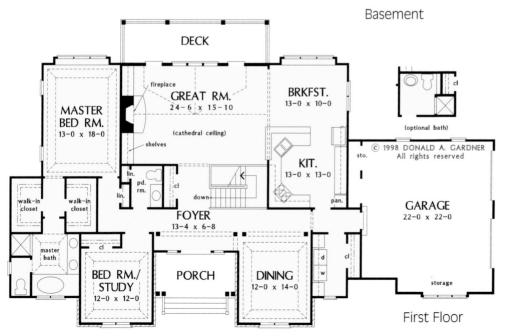

DECK

MASTER BED RM.
13-0 x 18-0

fireplace

GREAT RM.
24-6 x 15-10

(cathedral ceiling)

shelves

BRKFST.
13-0 x 10-0

walk-in closet

walk-in closet

master bath

lin.
pd. rm.
lin.
cl
down

KIT.
13-0 x 13-0

(optional bath)

cl

© 1998 DONALD A. GARDNER
All rights reserved

sto.

pan.

GARAGE
22-0 x 22-0

FOYER
13-4 x 6-8

BED RM./STUDY
12-0 x 12-0

PORCH

DINING
12-0 x 14-0

d w

cl

storage

First Floor

Rear Elevation

Donald A. Gardner Architects

Healthy Habitats

© 2002 Donald A. Gardner, Inc.

Brentwood
BHPDG01-998A
1-800-388-7580

3 Bedroom, 3 1/2 Bath

First Floor..............	1633 sq ft
Second Floor.........	751 sq ft
Total Living...........	2384 sq ft
Bonus...................	359 sq ft
Opt. Basement......	1633 sq ft
Width....................	69'8"
Depth...................	44'0"
Foundation..........	Basement or Crawl Space

PLAN PRICE SCHEDULE		
	Crawl	Basement
1 Set	$615	$865
4 Set	$665	$915
8 Set	$725	$975
Vellum	$925	$1,175

Rear Elevation

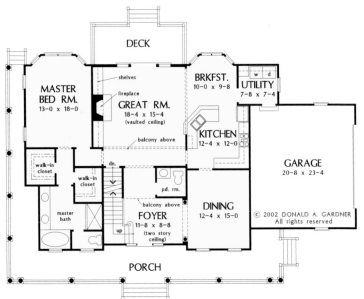

First Floor

Note: Basement floor plans not to scale.

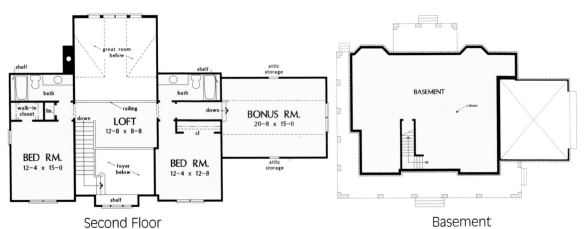

Second Floor

Basement

www.basementhomeplans.com

Donald A. Gardner Architects

Basement Tip

Choose fitness equipment based on the height of the person.

Edgewater
BHPDG01-1009A
1-800-388-7580

4 Bedroom, 3 Bath

First Floor.............. 2831 sq ft
Total Living........... 2831 sq ft
Opt. Basement...... 2917 sq ft
Width.................... 70'0"
Depth.................... 73'6"
Foundation........... Basement or Crawl Space

PLAN PRICE SCHEDULE		
	Crawl	Basement
1 Set	$660	$910
4 Set	$710	$960
8 Set	$770	$1,020
Vellum	$990	$1,240

FAMILY RM.
18-4 x 16-4
(cathedral ceiling)

fireplace

shelves

BRKFST.
9-8 x 12-6

DECK

SITTING
5-4 x 9-8

shelves

fireplace

niche

MASTER
BED RM.
13-4 x 16-4

bath

BED RM.
14-0 x 11-0

KITCHEN
13-4 x 13-4

LIVING RM.
20-0 x 20-2
(cathedral ceiling)

bath

cl

niche

lin.

walk-in
closet

walk-in
closet

UTIL.
6-0 x
11-4

FOYER
7-8 x
12-0

cl

walk-in
closet

BED RM.
14-0 x 11-4

DINING
12-0 x 15-0

BED RM./
STUDY
12-0 x 13-0

master
bath

d
w

down

seat

shelf

PORCH

GARAGE
22-8 x 22-0

storage

First Floor

Note: Basement floor plans not to scale.

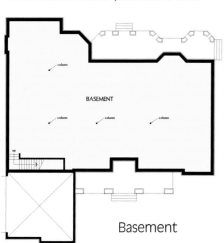

column

BASEMENT

column   column   column

up

Basement

2831
2917 BASEMENT
_____
5748 TOTAL

Rear Elevation

© 2002 Donald A. Gardner, Inc.

Madaridge
BHPDG01-974A
1-800-388-7580

3 Bedroom, 2 1/2 Bath

First Floor.............. 1527 sq ft
Second Floor........ 615 sq ft
Total Living........... 2142 sq ft
Bonus.................. 325 sq ft
Opt. Basement...... 1596 sq ft
Width.................. 40'4"
Depth.................. 73'8"
Foundation.......... Basement or
Crawl Space

PLAN PRICE SCHEDULE		
	Crawl	Basement
1 Set	$615	$865
4 Set	$665	$915
8 Set	$725	$975
Vellum	$925	$1,175

Rear Elevation

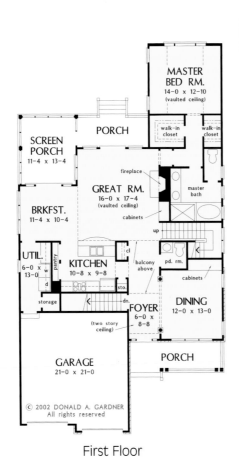

First Floor

© 2002 DONALD A. GARDNER
All rights reserved

Note: Basement floor plans not to scale.

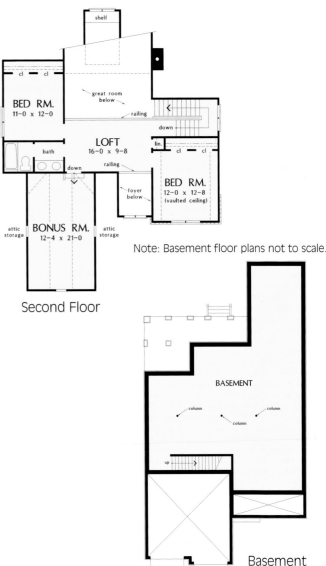

Second Floor

Basement

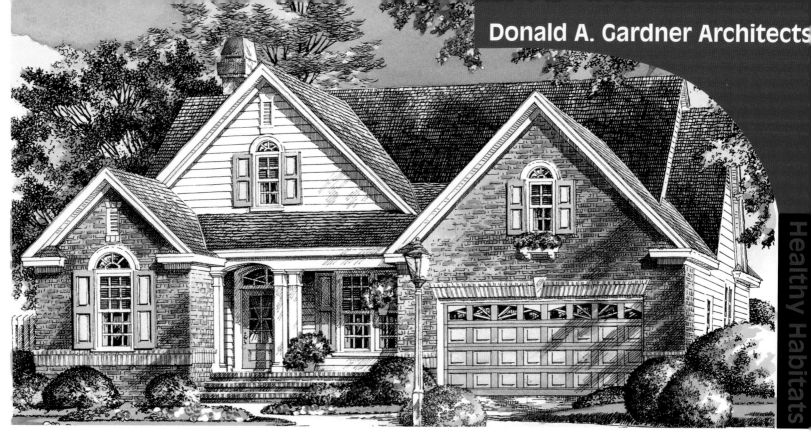

Healthy Habitats

© 2002 Donald A. Gardner, Inc.

Barrymore
BHPDG01-982A
1-800-388-7580

3 Bedroom, 2 Bath

First Floor............. 1665 sq ft
Total Living........... 1665 sq ft
Bonus.................. 404 sq ft
Opt. Basement...... 1739 sq ft
Width.................... 50'11"
Depth.................... 54'6"
Foundation........... Basement or Crawl Space

Bonus

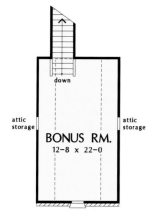

attic storage

down

BONUS RM.
12-8 x 22-0

attic storage

Bonus

Note: Basement floor plans not to scale.

BASEMENT

column

up

Basement

First Floor

DECK

BRKFST.
10-4 x 9-6

MASTER BED RM.
14-8 x 13-0
(vaulted ceiling)

walk in closet

fireplace

GREAT ROOM
17-6 x 15-6
(cathedral ceiling)

KIT.
10-0 x 11-8

UTIL.
6-0 x 14-0

master bath

up

w
d

seat

STUDY/ BED RM.
11-4 x 10-0

STORAGE

DINING
10-0 x 12-0

down

cl
cl
bath
lin

FOYER
6-0 x 18-0

GARAGE
21-0 x 22-0

cl

BED RM.
11-4 x 10-0
(vaulted ceiling)

PORCH

First Floor

PLAN PRICE SCHEDULE

	Crawl	Basement
1 Set	$570	$795
4 Set	$620	$845
8 Set	$680	$905
Vellum	$860	$1,085

Rear Elevation

Donald A. Gardner Architects

Healthy Habitats

© 2003 Donald A. Gardner, Inc.

Hilligan
BHPDG01-1015A
1-800-388-7580

3 Bedroom, 2 Bath

First Floor............. <u>1548 sq ft</u>
Total Living........... 1548 sq ft
Bonus.................... 406 sq ft
Opt. Basement...... 1631 sq ft
Width.................... 59'0"
Depth.................... 51'0"
Foundation.......... Basement or Crawl Space

PLAN PRICE SCHEDULE		
	Crawl	Basement
1 Set	$570	$795
4 Set	$620	$845
8 Set	$680	$905
Vellum	$860	$1,085

First Floor

MASTER BED RM.
15-8 x 13-0
(cathedral ceiling)

walk-in closet

master bath

seat

storage

KIT.
11-0 x 13-4

pan.

UTIL.
6-0 x 11-0

w

d

up

dn

DINING
11-0 x 12-0

PORCH

GREAT RM.
15-0 x 18-0
(cathedral ceiling)

fireplace

BED RM.
11-0 x 12-0

lin.

cl

bath

FOYER
5-0 x 5-0

cl

PORCH

BED RM./ STUDY
11-0 x 12-0
(cathedral ceiling)

GARAGE
21-0 x 22-0

Bonus

BONUS RM.
13-0 x 25-8

attic storage

attic storage

down

Basement Tip

Tumbling mats fold up nicely and are a great way to pad otherwise hard carpeting for the budding gymnast.

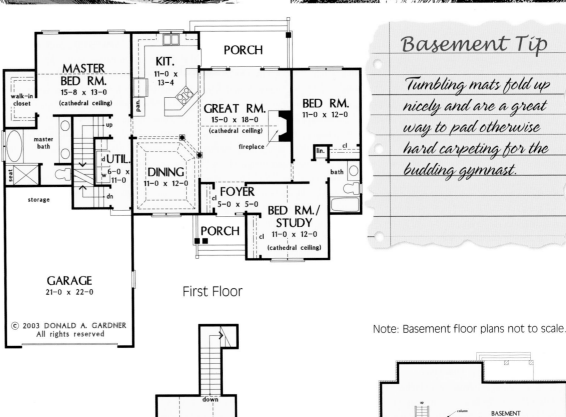

Note: Basement floor plans not to scale.

BASEMENT

up

column

BASEMENT FLOOR PLAN
PLAN NO. 1015A

Basement

Rear Elevation

Healthy Habitats

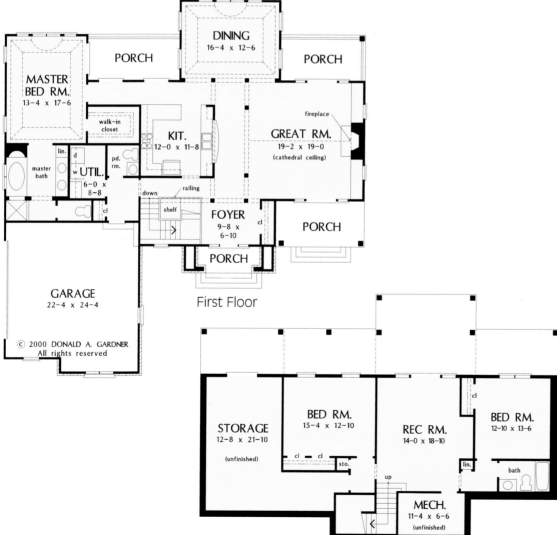

First Floor

DINING
16–4 x 12–6

PORCH

PORCH

MASTER
BED RM.
13–4 x 17–6

walk-in
closet

KIT.
12–0 x 11–8

GREAT RM.
19–2 x 19–0
(cathedral ceiling)

fireplace

lin.

master
bath

d
w UTIL.
6–0 x
8–8

pd.
rm.

down

railing

shelf

cl

FOYER
9–8 x
6–10

cl

PORCH

PORCH

GARAGE
22–4 x 24–4

Basement

STORAGE
12–8 x 21–10
(unfinished)

BED RM.
15–4 x 12–10

cl   cl

sto.

REC RM.
14–0 x 18–10

up

MECH.
11–4 x 6–6
(unfinished)

cl

BED RM.
12–10 x 13–6

lin.

bath

Highlands
BHPDG01-852D
1-800-388-7580

3 Bedroom, 2 1/2 Bath
First Floor.............. 1694 sq ft
Basement.............. <u>971 sq ft</u>
Total Living........... 2665 sq ft
Width..................... 60'6"
Depth.....................61'2"
Foundation...........Hillside
Walkout

PLAN PRICE SCHEDULE	
	Walkout
1 Set	$660
4 Set	$710
8 Set	$770
Vellum	$990

Rear Elevation

© 2003 Donald A. Gardner, Inc.

Jarrell
BHPDG01-1017A
1-800-388-7580

3 Bedroom, 2 Bath

First Floor.............. 1741 sq ft
Total Living........... 1741 sq ft
Bonus.................... 398 sq ft
Opt. Basement...... 1804 sq ft
Width................... 46'0"
Depth................... 70'0"
Foundation.......... Basement or Crawl Space

PLAN PRICE SCHEDULE		
	Crawl	Basement
1 Set	$570	$795
4 Set	$620	$845
8 Set	$680	$905
Vellum	$860	$1,085

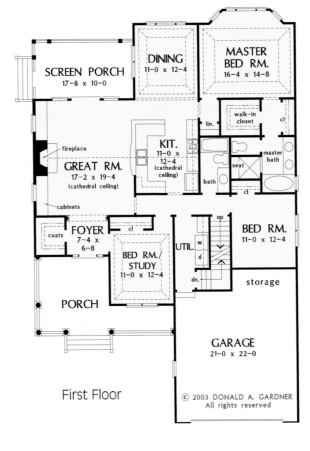

First Floor

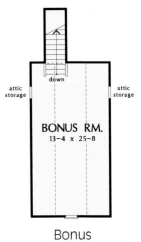

Bonus

Note: Basement floor plans not to scale.

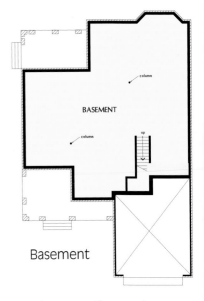

Basement

Rear Elevation

Healthy Habitats

handwritten notes:

1803
80
―――
1883
918   NO BASEMENT
―――
2801
1803
―――
4604   TOTAL

63
63
57
57
―――
240 linear

Liberty Hill
BHPDG01-414A
1-800-388-7580

3 Bedroom, 2 Bath

First Floor............. 1803 sq ft
Second Floor........ <u>80 sq ft</u>
Total Living........... 1883 sq ft
Bonus.................. 918 sq ft
Opt. Basement...... 1803 sq ft
Width.................... 63'8"
Depth.................... 57'4"
Foundation........... Basement or Crawl Space

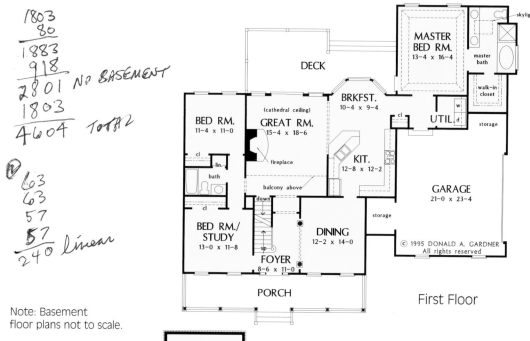

First Floor

MASTER BED RM.
13-4 x 16-4

DECK

BRKFST.
10-4 x 9-4

master bath

walk-in closet

skylight

UTIL.

storage

GREAT RM.
15-4 x 18-6
(cathedral ceiling)

BED RM.
11-4 x 11-0

fireplace

KIT.
12-8 x 12-2

GARAGE
21-0 x 23-4

balcony above

BED RM./
STUDY
13-0 x 11-8

DINING
12-2 x 14-0

FOYER
8-6 x 11-0

storage

PORCH

Note: Basement floor plans not to scale.

PLAN PRICE SCHEDULE		
	Crawl	Basement
1 Set	$570	$795
4 Set	$620	$845
8 Set	$680	$905
Vellum	$860	$1,085

Basement

BASEMENT

column   column

up

Second Floor

great room below

attic storage

railing

attic storage

BONUS
13-0 x 18-6
(unfinished)

down

sto.

foyer below

BONUS
12-2 x 10-10
(unfinished)

attic storage

skylights

Rear Elevation

Healthy Habitats

Photographed home may have been modified
from the original construction documents.

Wyndham
BHPDG01-793A
1-800-388-7580

4 Bedroom, 3 Bath

First Floor.............. 1668 sq ft
Second Floor........ 495 sq ft
Total Living........... 2163 sq ft
Bonus.................... 327 sq ft
Opt. Basement...... 1668 sq ft
Width.................... 52'7"
Depth.................... 50'11"
Foundation.......... Basement or
                      Crawl Space

(handwritten calculations)

1668
495
2163
327
2490 NO BASEMENT
1668
4158 TOTAL

52
50
50
52
204 LINEAR FEET

PLAN PRICE SCHEDULE		
	Crawl	Basement
1 Set	$615	$865
4 Set	$665	$915
8 Set	$725	$975
Vellum	$925	$1,175

Second Floor

BED RM.
11-0 x 12-0

BED RM.
11-0 x 13-10
(vaulted ceiling)

BONUS RM.
15-4 x 21-4

great room below

walk-in closet

foyer below

Note: Basement floor plans not to scale.

DECK

(vaulted ceiling)

GREAT RM.
16-8 x 17-10

BRKFST.
11-4 x 9-0

MASTER BED RM.
15-8 x 13-4

fireplace

KIT.
11-4 x 12-8

walk-in closet

lin.

UTIL.
7-10 x 6-8

master bath

bath

STUDY/ BED RM.
11-0 x 12-0

FOYER
5-4 x 12-0

DINING
11-4 x 12-0

GARAGE
22-4 x 21-4

storage

PORCH

First Floor

BASEMENT
column
up

Basement

Rear Elevation

First Floor

(handwritten notes)
2237 1st FLOOR
1182 2ND FLOOR
3419
475 BONUS
3894 NO BASEMENT
2247
6141 TOTAL
85
85
56
56
282 linear

© 2002 Donald A. Gardner, Inc.

Yesterview
BHPDG01-1002A
1-800-388-7580

4 Bedroom, 3 1/2 Bath

First Floor............. 2237 sq ft
Second Floor......... 1182 sq ft
Total Living........... 3419 sq ft
Bonus.................. 475 sq ft
Opt. Basement...... 2247 sq ft
Width.................. 85'4"
Depth.................. 56'4"
Foundation........... Basement or Crawl Space

PLAN PRICE SCHEDULE		
	Crawl	Basement
1 Set	$705	$980
4 Set	$755	$1,030
8 Set	$815	$1,090
Vellum	$1,055	$1,330

Second Floor

Note: Basement floor plans not to scale.

Basement

Rear Elevation

USEFUL

SPACES

The utility room has traditionally been a place to wash clothes, leave dirty shoes or check the hot water heater. Today, utility rooms are replacing arid alcoves with a space that livens up laundry and transforms the room into a favorite multi-purpose domain. Perfect for an artist's gallery or mechanic's workshop, a utility room enables the most obscure project room to flourish.

Utility room lighting is key. In most indoor rooms it is a rule of thumb to avoid fluorescent lighting, but in the utility room it is strongly suggested. Whether you need extra light to help you see stains on clothes or to thread a needle, the added illumination will enhance even the smallest details.

...Underground Utility

Built-in furniture also deserves some consideration. Cabinetry creates an overhead storage space for detergent or potting soil. Depending on your craft, large counter space with multiple drawers for nails, pins or fabrics will help keep clutter to a minimum. Adding a sofa or built-in bench creates a relaxing area to lounge when folding clothes or brainstorming a project.

If you're a green thumb or have large pets, consider installing a large, deep sink. Perfect for grooming oversized houseplants, pre-treating stains or washing the dog, a large sink makes these tasks much easier than dirtying the bathtub or trying to fight with dishes.

Since your utility room won't have many visitors, get creative with decorations and furnishings. Go crazy with bold colors or old pictures, and make it a fun place to get work done. Radios and coffee makers are great extras to help pass the time and promote comfort.

The basement is no longer just for laundry or unused storage space. Families are using the area to work on that old car, paint their masterpiece, or build the next great invention. However you choose to utilize this abundant space, make your utility room a colorful, comfortable place to work.

ENCHANTING VISTA

Above: The large master bath features dual sinks, a grand arched window and recessed lighting for an enchanting look.

Left: With an abundance of windows, the rear is equally as stunning as the front exterior.

Above: The master bedroom's sitting area includes multiple over-sized windows for an invigorating view.

Featuring a rear exterior equally as striking as the front, the *Cedar Court* combines elegant living with a practical floor plan. With romantic arches and masterful peaks, this home reflects sophistication in every detail. The roofline mimics the natural relationship of mountains and valleys with its pitches, and an extraordinary rear wall of windows frame breathtaking views. Spacious porches beckon enchanting breezes, while a screened porch with a stone fireplace allows four-season enjoyment.

Left: A generous stone fireplace becomes a stunning focal point in the great room.

Right: Rich textures and neutral-colored furniture accent the hardwood floors and natural elements throughout the home.

The first floor is overwhelmingly open. Columns decoratively designate the borders of the dining room, while the kitchen, breakfast and great room all gracefully flow into one another. A hexagonal screened porch with fireplace creates the perfect area for enjoying alfresco meals. Tray ceilings crown the dining room, study and master bedroom, adding vertical volume and ornate detail to each.

The large master bedroom includes an additional sitting area hugged by a bay window, as well as a luxurious master bath. Dual vanities and a private privy grant simplicity in daily rituals, and the generous walk-in closet provides ample room for two wardrobes.

Above: Providing convenience, the cooktop island enables several workstations in the kitchen.

Just off the garage are the powder and utility rooms, promoting convenience for last-minute glances in the mirror or retrieving muddy shoes. A perfect home office, the versatile study is privately situated from other living rooms for increased work productivity.

The basement level includes two additional bedrooms, each with their own private baths separated by an expansive covered patio. The rec room features a second fireplace, but also noteworthy are the two unfinished storage areas. The larger of the two makes a perfect workshop or hobby/craft room. Designed to grow with you, the storage rooms can be used to expand the living areas of the basement level or house your favorite project.

Below: Wooden columns punctuate the breakfast room and enhance the open layout.

With an alluring exterior and matching interior, the *Cedar Court's* flexible floor plan is ideal for today's expanding families.

Left: Accented by a tray ceiling and sitting area, the master bedroom lives even larger than its size indicates.

Below: Stone and stucco combine with multiple gables and a large dormer to provide the ultimate curb appeal.

Cedar Court

BHPAL01-5004

3 Bedroom, 3 1/2 Bath
First Floor......... 2446 sq ft
Basement......... 1374 sq ft
Total Living....... 3820 sq ft
Width.............. 82' 4"
Depth.............. 95' 10"
Foundation...... Hillside
Walkout

1-800-388-7580

www.basementhomeplans.com

Please Note: Home photographed may differ from actual construction documents.

PLAN PRICE SCHEDULE	
	Walkout
Vellum	Call For Custom Pricing

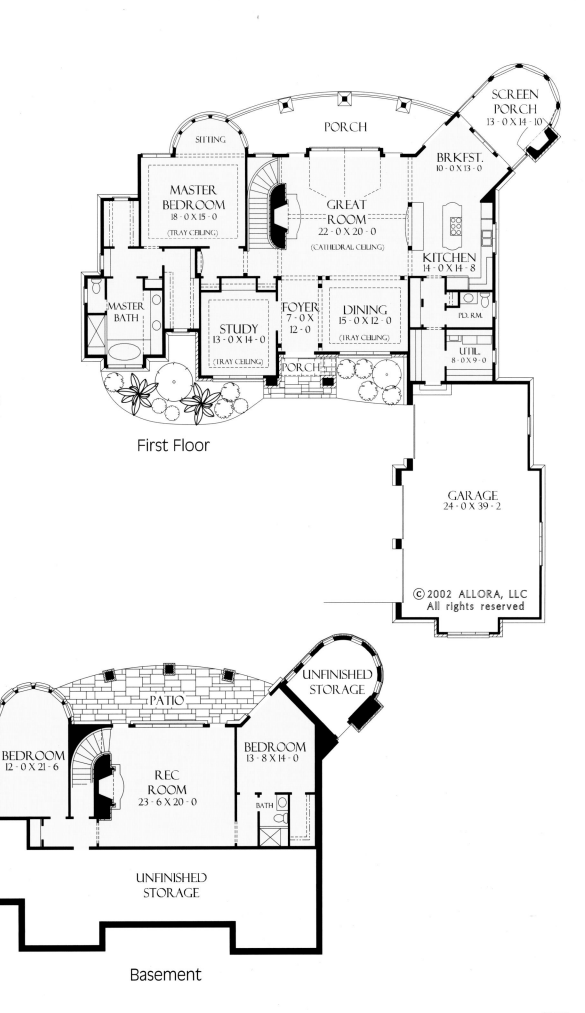

First Floor

Basement

Above: With Georgian-inspired details, this stately home sparks instant curb appeal.

© 2000 Donald A. Gardner, Inc.

CLASSIC COMFORT

French doors and transoms flank the great room's focal point—the stately fireplace.

This home's commanding brick exterior with arched keystones, quoins, covered entry and hip roof create a stunning presence, while the **Santerini's** spacious interior is equally impressive.

An exciting second-floor balcony overlooks the vaulted foyer and great room. French doors flank the great

room's fireplace and lead to the back porch and patio. The adjacent kitchen is generously proportioned, featuring a sizable work island and nearby built-in desk and walk-in pantry. A short hall provides extra privacy for the first-floor master suite, which enjoys a tray ceiling, fireplace, back-porch access, his-and-her walk-in closets and bath with garden tub.

The open basement level lends itself naturally as an artist's or crafter's haven.

The Santerini blends a traditional look with a modern floor plan for a truly impeccable home.

Basement Tip

✔ Adding a phone line in the basement keeps trips upstairs to a minimum and enables you to never miss a call.

Above: Twin chimneys and dormers create an impressive rear exterior.

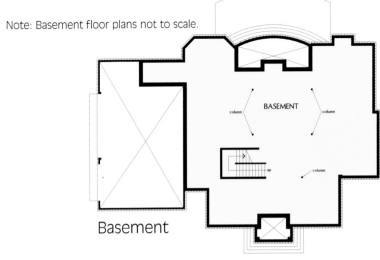

Note: Basement floor plans not to scale.

Rear Elevation

Basement

Santerini

BHPDG01-868A

3 Bedroom, 2 1/2 Bath

First Floor.......... 2270 sq ft

Second Floor..... <u>685 sq ft</u>

Total Living......... 2955 sq ft

Bonus................ 563 sq ft

Opt. Basement.. 2281 sq ft

Width................. 75' 1"

Depth................ 53' 6"

Foundation...... Basement or Crawl Space

1-800-388-7580

www.basementhomeplans.com

Please Note: Home photographed may differ from actual construction documents.

PLAN PRICE SCHEDULE		
	Crawl	Basement
1 Set	$660	$910
4 Set	$710	$960
8 Set	$770	$1,020
Vellum	$990	$1,240

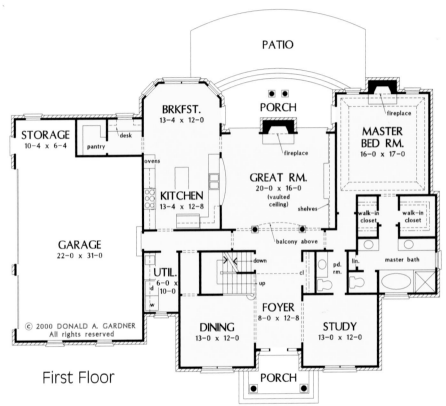

First Floor

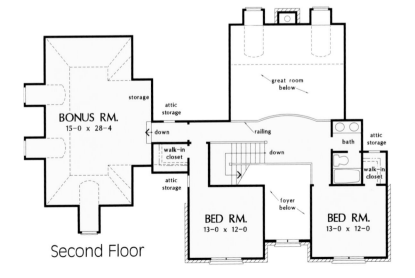

Second Floor

HILLSIDE HANGOUT

Cedar shake, stone and siding embellish the sophisticated exterior of the **Monte Vista**. This European-styled sloping-lot home features an expansive deck that allows for spectacular rear views.

Ceiling treatments enhance the open living and dining rooms as well as the versatile bedroom/study. The kitchen features a favorable layout with center cooktop island and adjoining breakfast bay with rear-deck access. Three bedrooms and three baths are located on the first floor, including a lovely master suite with French door-access to the spacious rear deck.

Above: Wooden cabinetry, French doors and bay windows create a striking blend with the warm-colored hardwood floors.

Left: Dual porches expand the back of the home, melding indoors with the outdoors.

The generous basement level not only includes two bedrooms and multiple bathrooms, but also a large family room that could function perfectly as a handyman's retreat. The wall opposite the fireplace is the ultimate place for a workbench, and as an underground workshop, louder tools are muted from the rooms upstairs. For all the odd jobs around the house, a basement workshop provides a spacious way to fix most family repairs.

Below: Transoms and oversized windows enhance the open living room, which gently flows into the kitchen.

www.basementhomeplans.com

DECK

KIT.
11-10 x 14-0

BRKFST.
10-0 x 14-0

LIVING RM.
16-4 x 20-0
fireplace
(cathedral ceiling)

MASTER
BED RM.
17-0 x 14-0

down

railing

linen

master
bath

cl

bath

DINING
13-0 x 14-4

FOYER
6-8 x
13-2

lin.

walk-in
closet

cl

BED RM.
12-0 x 13-0

cl

cl

UTIL.
7-4 x
9-0

d
w

bath

storage

BED RM./
STUDY
13-0 x 13-0

PORCH

GARAGE
22-0 x 22-8

First Floor

Above: Multiple gables and a single dormer give this home an intriguing exterior.

COVERED
PATIO

BED RM.
13-8 x 14-0

bath

cl

cl

cl

pd.
rm.

FAMILY RM.
16-4 x 20-0
fireplace

cl

cl

lin.

BED RM.
14-8 x 12-4

bath

storage

up

STORAGE
(unfinished)

Basement

Monte Vista
BHPDG01-711D

5 Bedroom, 5 1/2 Bath
First Floor......... 2297 sq ft
Basement......... 1212 sq ft
Total Living....... 3509 sq ft
Width.............. 70' 10"
Depth.............. 69' 0"
Foundation...... Hillside
          Walkout

1-800-388-7580
www.basementhomeplans.com

Please Note: Home photographed may differ from actual construction documents.

PLAN PRICE SCHEDULE	
	Walkout
1 Set	$775
4 Set	$825
8 Set	$885
Vellum	$1,135

© 1999 Donald A. Gardner, Inc.

NATURAL BEAUTY

Designed for sloping lots, the *Ryecroft* positions its common living areas and master suite on the first floor. With a bay window and back-porch access, the master suite boasts dual walk-in closets and a luxurious bath. The kitchen is open to multiple rooms, and the breakfast area features a nearby walk-in pantry.

Above: Multiple transoms and French doors raise the eye to a striking clerestory window accented by vaulted ceilings.

Left: Arches abound on the covered front porch and complement the gable peaks on the façade of this stylish Craftsman home.

The basement features two bedrooms and baths that flank the open rec room. For garden lovers, this open space could work naturally as a place to groom both indoor and outdoor houseplants. The wet bar provides an ideal watering station, while built-in cabinetry creates a stylish way to store plant food, gloves and trimming tools. Green thumbs alike will enjoy the added space for projects.

Ryecroft

BHPDG01-824D

3 Bedroom, 3 1/2 Bath
First Floor......... 1725 sq ft
Basement......... <u>1090 sq ft</u>
Total Living....... 2815 sq ft
Width.............. 59' 0"
Depth.............. 59' 4"
Foundation...... Hillside
Walkout

1-800-388-7580

www.basementhomeplans.com

Please Note: Home photographed may differ from actual construction documents.

PLAN PRICE SCHEDULE	
	Walkout
1 Set	$660
4 Set	$710
8 Set	$770
Vellum	$990

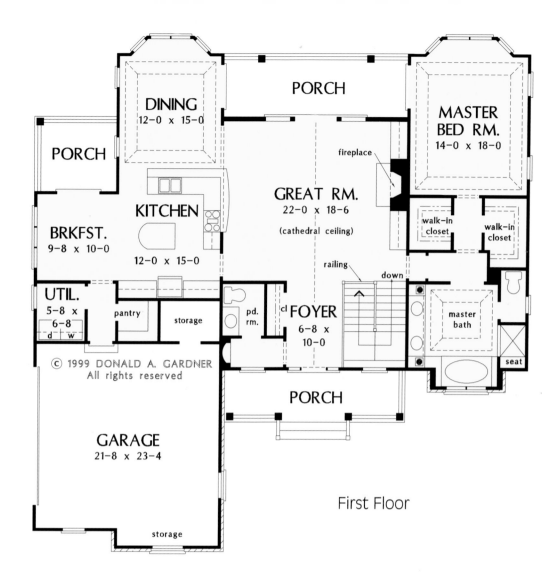

First Floor

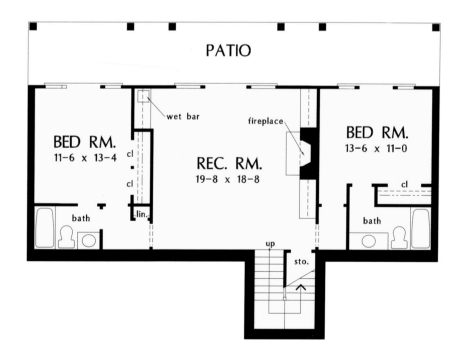

Basement

Donald A. Gardner Architects

© 1994 Donald A. Gardner Architects, Inc.

Ingraham
BHPDG01-332A
1-800-388-7580

3 Bedroom, 2 Bath

First Floor............. 2025 sq ft
Total Living........... 2025 sq ft
Bonus.................... 433 sq ft
Opt. Basement...... 2079 sq ft
Width................... 69'8"
Depth................... 63'10"
Foundation.......... Basement or
Crawl Space

PLAN PRICE SCHEDULE		
	Crawl	Basement
1 Set	$570	$795
4 Set	$620	$845
8 Set	$680	$905
Vellum	$860	$1,085

First Floor

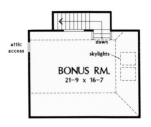

Bonus

Note: Basement floor plans not to scale.

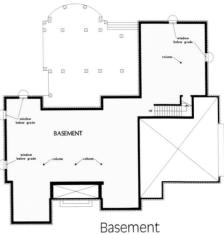

Basement

Rear Elevation

Photographed home may have been modified from the original construction documents.

www.basementhomeplans.com

© 1999 Donald A. Gardner, Inc.

Dakota
BHPDG01-789D
1-800-388-7580

4 Bedroom, 3 Bath

First Floor..............	2105 sq ft
Basement..............	811 sq ft
Total Living...........	2916 sq ft
Bonus...................	453 sq ft
Width...................	61'8"
Depth...................	67'4"
Foundation..........	Hillside Walkout

DECK

MASTER BED RM. 13-0 x 18-0

fireplace

GREAT RM. 22-0 x 15-10 (cathedral ceiling)

BRKFST. 13-0 x 10-0

KITCHEN 13-0 x 12-0

BED RM. 12-0 x 12-8

bath

walk-in closet

lin.

walk-in closet

railing

down

FOYER 5-8 x 9-0

DINING 12-0 x 14-8

d w

cl

up

BED RM. 12-0 x 11-0

cl

master bath

PORCH

GARAGE 22-0 x 25-4

First Floor

Note: Basement floor plans not to scale.

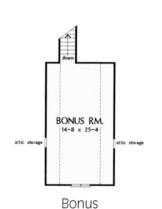

down

BONUS RM. 14-8 x 25-4

attic storage   attic storage

Bonus

PLAN PRICE SCHEDULE	
	Walkout
1 Set	$660
4 Set	$710
8 Set	$770
Vellum	$990

PATIO

(unfinished) **STORAGE** 12-8 x 15-10

REC. ROOM 22-0 x 15-9

BED RM. 13-0 x 14-0

cl

bath

cl

up

Basement

Rear Elevation

Useful Spaces

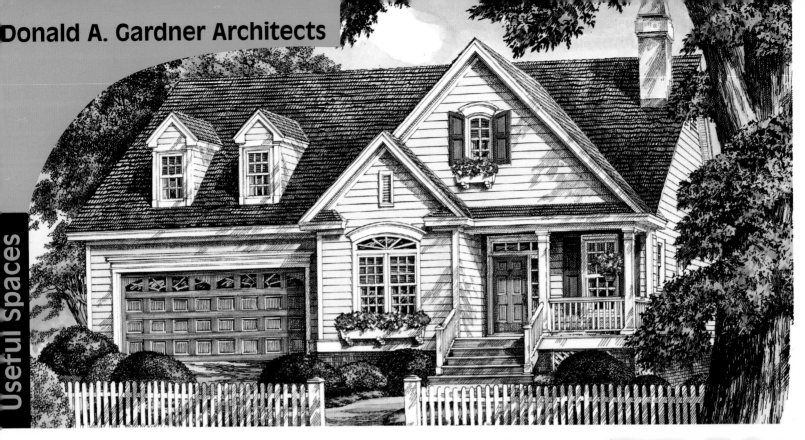

Tolliver
BHPDG01-859A
1-800-388-7580

3 Bedroom, 2 Bath

First Floor..............	1250 sq ft
Total Living...........	1250 sq ft
Bonus....................	524 sq ft
Opt. Basement......	1337 sq ft
Width....................	47'0"
Depth....................	41'
Foundation..........	Basement or Crawl Space

PLAN PRICE SCHEDULE		
	Crawl	Basement
1 Set	$525	$750
4 Set	$575	$800
8 Set	$635	$860
Vellum	$795	$1,020

First Floor

MASTER BED RM. 14-0 x 11-0 (cathedral ceiling)
walk-in closet
master bath
storage
GARAGE 21-0 x 21-0
BED RM. 11-0 x 11-0
BED RM. 11-4 x 11-0
bath
KIT. 11-0 x 9-4
GREAT RM. 13-8 x 16-0 (cathedral ceiling) fireplace
DINING 11-0 x 13-0
PORCH

Basement Tip

Bathing the dog after a muddy run in the park is easier in a deep sink.

Note: Basement floor plans not to scale.

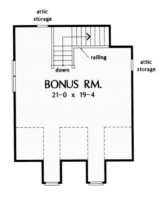

attic storage
BONUS RM. 21-0 x 19-4
railing
down
attic storage

Bonus

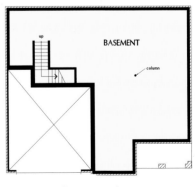

up
BASEMENT
column

Basement

Rear Elevation

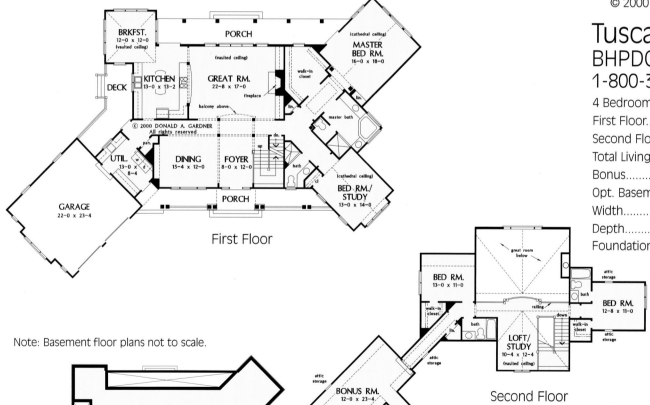

BRKFST. 12-0 x 12-0 (vaulted ceiling)

PORCH

MASTER BED RM. 16-0 x 18-0 (cathedral ceiling)

KITCHEN 13-0 x 13-2

DECK

(vaulted ceiling)

GREAT RM. 22-8 x 17-0

walk-in closet

fireplace

lin.

balcony above

master bath

lin.

UTIL. 13-0 x 8-4

pan.

DINING 15-4 x 12-0

FOYER 8-0 x 12-0

up dn.

bath

GARAGE 22-0 x 23-4

PORCH

(cathedral ceiling)

BED RM./ STUDY 13-0 x 14-0

cl.

First Floor

Note: Basement floor plans not to scale.

BASEMENT

column

column

up

Basement

© 2000 Donald A. Gardner, Inc.

Tuscany
BHPDG01-877A
1-800-388-7580

4 Bedroom, 4 Bath

First Floor............. 2477 sq ft
Second Floor......... 742 sq ft
Total Living........... 3219 sq ft
Bonus.................. 419 sq ft
Opt. Basement...... 2485 sq ft
Width................... 99'10"
Depth................... 66'2"
Foundation........... Basement or Crawl Space

great room below

BED RM. 13-0 x 11-0

attic storage

bath

BED RM. 12-8 x 11-0

walk-in closet

lin.

bath

railing

down

walk-in closet

attic storage

LOFT/ STUDY 10-4 x 12-4 (vaulted ceiling)

attic storage

attic storage

BONUS RM. 12-0 x 23-4

Second Floor

PLAN PRICE SCHEDULE		
	Crawl	Basement
1 Set	$705	$980
4 Set	$755	$1,030
8 Set	$815	$1,090
Vellum	$1055	$1,330

Rear Elevation

Donald A. Gardner Architects

Useful Spaces

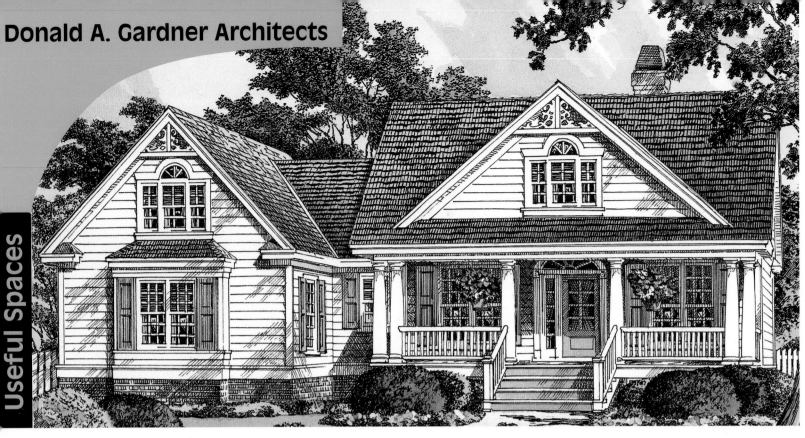

© 2003 Donald A. Gardner, Inc.

Violet
BHPDG01-1016A
1-800-388-7580

3 Bedroom, 2 Bath

First Floor	1674 sq ft
Total Living	1674 sq ft
Bonus	418 sq ft
Opt. Basement	1760 sq ft
Width	65'4"
Depth	52'4"
Foundation	Basement or Crawl Space

PLAN PRICE SCHEDULE		
	Crawl	Basement
1 Set	$570	$795
4 Set	$620	$845
8 Set	$680	$905
Vellum	$860	$1,085

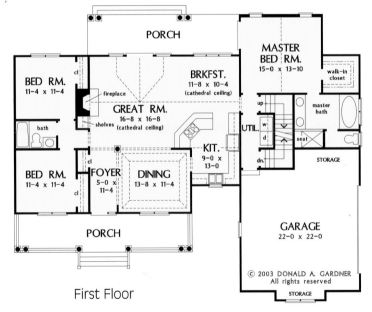

First Floor

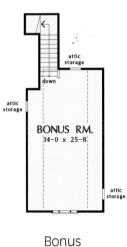

Bonus

Note: Basement floor plans not to scale.

Rear Elevation

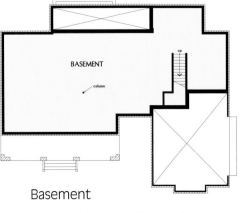

Basement

www.basementhomeplans.com

Useful Spaces

handwritten notes:
1817
425 BONUS
————
2242 NO BASEMENT
1883
————
4125 TOTAL

Georgetown
BHPDG01-393A
1-800-388-7580

3 Bedroom, 2 Bath

First Floor............... <u>1817 sq ft</u>
Total Living............ 1817 sq ft
Bonus.................... 425 sq ft
Opt. Basement...... 1883 sq ft
Width.................... 65'4"
Depth.................... 62'0"
Foundation........... Basement or Crawl Space

First Floor

MASTER BED RM. 14-0 x 16-4
master bath
walk-in closet
skylight
up
w d
UTIL.
down
storage
PORCH
BRKFST. 11-4 x 9-2
(cathedral ceiling)
BED RM. 12-8 x 11-0
GREAT RM. 16-4 x 18-8
fireplace
cl
lin.
bath
walk-in closet
KIT. 11-4 x 12-4
© 1995 DONALD A. GARDNER All rights reserved
GARAGE 21-8 x 22-4
storage
cl
BED RM./ STUDY 12-4 x 13-0
FOYER 6-4 x 9-8
vaulted ceiling
DINING 12-4 x 13-0
(optional door location)
PORCH

Note: Basement floor plans not to scale.

BASEMENT
up
column
column

Basement

attic storage
storage
down
skylights
BONUS RM. 12-8 x 22-4

Bonus

PLAN PRICE SCHEDULE		
	Crawl	Basement
1 Set	$570	$795
4 Set	$620	$845
8 Set	$680	$905
Vellum	$860	$1,085

Rear Elevation

Useful Spaces

Dewfield
BHPDG01-1030A
1-800-388-7580

3 Bedroom, 2 Bath

First Floor.............	1724 sq ft
Total Living...........	1724 sq ft
Bonus..................	327 sq ft
Opt. Basement......	1753 sq ft
Width..................	56'8"
Depth..................	48'4"
Foundation..........	Basement or Crawl Space

PLAN PRICE SCHEDULE		
	Crawl	Basement
1 Set	$570	$795
4 Set	$620	$845
8 Set	$680	$905
Vellum	$860	$1,085

1724
327
2051 NO BASEMENT
1753
3804 TOTAL

Rear Elevation

First Floor

PORCH

KIT.
9-4 x 12-0

DINING
12-8 x 12-0

GREAT RM.
16-0 x 18-10
(cathedral ceiling)

fireplace

MASTER
BED RM.
17-4 x 12-4

walk-in closet

linen

master bath

lin.

UTIL.
6-4 x 6-0

pantry   desk

dn.

up

FOYER
8-0 x 9-0

bath

shelf

GARAGE
22-0 x 22-0

PORCH

BED RM.
11-4 x 12-0
(vaulted ceiling)

BED RM.
11-4 x 12-0

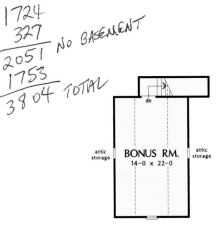

attic storage

BONUS RM.
14-0 x 22-0

attic storage

dn

Bonus

Basement Tip

Hang pictures in the basement slightly lower than you would on other floors of the house so ceilings appear taller.

Note: Basement floor plans not to scale.

column

BASEMENT

column

up

Basement

www.basementhomeplans.com

Useful Spaces

First Floor

PORCH

DINING
12-0 x 14-4

SCREEN PORCH
10-0 x 11-8

MASTER BED RM.
14-0 x 16-0

GREAT RM.
21-0 x 15-10
(vaulted ceiling)
fireplace
balcony above

KITCHEN
12-0 x 14-2

BRKFST.
10-0 x 10-0

walk-in closet

master bath

FOYER
6-8 x 7-7

UTILITY
8-4 x 5-8

PORCH

GARAGE
22-0 x 24-0

STORAGE
14-0 x 11-10

Second Floor

BED RM.
11-8 x 13-0

great room below

railing

foyer below

BED RM.
11-8 x 12-0

bath

attic storage

attic storage

BONUS RM.
13-2 x 31-0

Basement

PATIO

STORAGE
13-4 x 15-6
(unfinished)

FAMILY RM.
17-10 x 15-4
fireplace

BED RM./ STUDY
12-0 x 10-0
wet bar
bath

Rockledge
BHPDG01-875D
1-800-388-7580

4 Bedroom, 3 1/2 Bath

First Floor	1682 sq ft
Second Floor	577 sq ft
Basement	690 sq ft
Total Living	2949 sq ft
Bonus	459 sq ft
Width	79'0"
Depth	68'2"
Foundation	Hillside Walkout

PLAN PRICE SCHEDULE	
	Walkout
1 Set	$660
4 Set	$710
8 Set	$770
Vellum	$990

Rear Elevation

Note: Basement floor plans not to scale.

Useful Spaces

Southerland
BHPDG01-971A
1-800-388-7580

4 Bedroom, 3 1/2 Bath

First Floor............. 1798 sq ft
Second Floor......... 723 sq ft
Total Living........... 2521 sq ft
Bonus.................. 349 sq ft
Opt. Basement...... 1798 sq ft
Width.................. 66'8"
Depth.................. 49'8"
Foundation.......... Basement or Crawl Space

PLAN PRICE SCHEDULE		
	Crawl	Basement
1 Set	$660	$910
4 Set	$710	$960
8 Set	$770	$1,020
Vellum	$990	$1,240

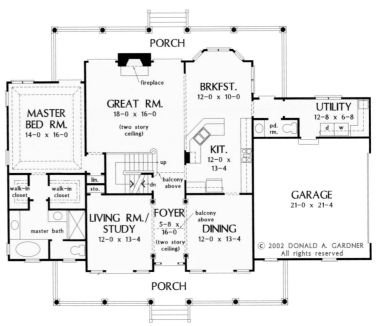

First Floor

Rear Elevation

Second Floor

Note: Basement floor plans not to scale.

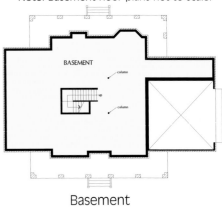

Basement

Useful Spaces

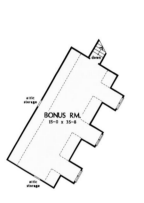

Bonus

BONUS RM.
15-0 x 35-8

attic storage

First Floor

© 2001 Donald A. Gardner
All rights reserved

© 2001 Donald A. Gardner, Inc.

Cedar Creek
BHPDG01-959A
1-800-388-7580

3 Bedroom, 2 1/2 Bath

First Floor..............	3214 sq ft
Total Living...........	3214 sq ft
Bonus..................	615 sq ft
Opt. Basement......	3265 sq ft
Width..................	108'
Depth..................	107' 7"
Foundation...........	Basement or Crawl Space

PLAN PRICE SCHEDULE		
	Crawl	Basement
1 Set	$705	$980
4 Set	$755	$1,030
8 Set	$815	$1,090
Vellum	$1055	$1,330

Note: Basement floor plans not to scale.

Basement

Rear Elevation

© 1998 Donald A. Gardner, Inc.

Indigo
BHPDG01-727A
1-800-388-7580

3 Bedroom, 3 Bath

First Floor............. 2280 sq ft
Total Living........... 2280 sq ft
Opt. Basement...... 2314 sq ft
Width.................... 69'6"
Depth.................... 59'6"
Foundation.......... Basement or Crawl Space

PLAN PRICE SCHEDULE		
	Crawl	Basement
1 Set	$615	$865
4 Set	$665	$915
8 Set	$725	$975
Vellum	$925	$1,175

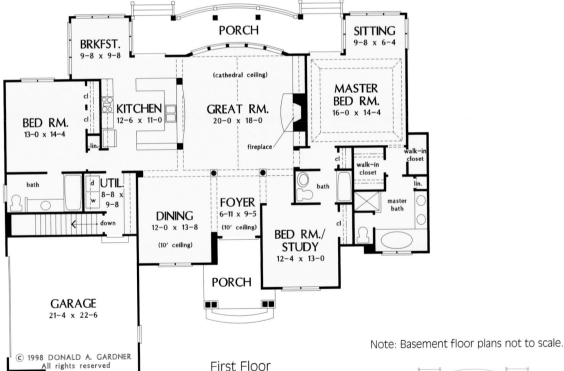

First Floor

BRKFST.
9-8 x 9-8

PORCH

SITTING
9-8 x 6-4

KITCHEN
12-6 x 11-0

GREAT RM.
20-0 x 18-0

(cathedral ceiling)

MASTER BED RM.
16-0 x 14-4

BED RM.
13-0 x 14-4

fireplace

walk-in closet

bath

UTIL.
8-8 x 9-8

DINING
12-0 x 13-8

(10' ceiling)

FOYER
6-11 x 9-5

(10' ceiling)

bath

walk-in closet

master bath

BED RM./STUDY
12-4 x 13-0

PORCH

GARAGE
21-4 x 22-6

Note: Basement floor plans not to scale.

BASEMENT

column   column   column

Basement

Rear Elevation

Photographed home may have been modified from the original construction documents.

Donald A. Gardner Architects

BONUS RM
14-10 x 25-8
(cathedral ceiling)

attic storage

attic storage

down

Bonus

MASTER BED RM.
14-8 x 17-0

walk-in closet

walk-in closet

lin.

master bath

UTIL.
7-4 x 7-0

storage

BRKFST.
10-0 x 9-0

KIT.
11-4 x 13-4

DINING
13-0 x 11-0

skylights

PORCH

GREAT RM.
19-0 x 17-0
(cathedral ceiling)

wet bar

shelves

fireplace

FOYER
6-4 x 11-0

up

dn

GARAGE
22-0 x 22-0

PORCH

BED RM.
11-0 x 13-0

BED RM.
13-0 x 11-0

cl

bath

BED RM./
STUDY
11-0 x 13-0

cl

cl

storage

First Floor

© 2003 Donald A. Gardner, Inc.

Lilycrest
BHPDG01-1022A
1-800-388-7580

4 Bedroom, 2 Bath

First Floor.............. 2261 sq ft
Total Living........... 2261 sq ft
Bonus.................... 395 sq ft
Opt. Basement...... 2316 sq ft
Width.................... 62'0"
Depth....................70'10"
Foundation...........Basement or Crawl Space

PLAN PRICE SCHEDULE		
	Crawl	Basement
1 Set	$615	$865
4 Set	$665	$915
8 Set	$725	$975
Vellum	$925	$1,175

Note: Basement floor plans not to scale.

column

BASEMENT

column

column

up

Basement

Rear Elevation

© 2001 Donald A. Gardner, Inc.

Kerwin
BHPDG01-913A
1-800-388-7580

4 Bedroom, 2 Bath

First Floor............. 2508 sq ft
Total Living........... 2508 sq ft
Bonus.................. 446 sq ft
Opt. Basement...... 2587 sq ft
Width.................. 71'2"
Depth.................. 70'10"
Foundation.......... Basement or Crawl Space

PLAN PRICE SCHEDULE		
	Crawl	Basement
1 Set	$615	$865
4 Set	$665	$915
8 Set	$725	$975
Vellum	$925	$1,175

First Floor

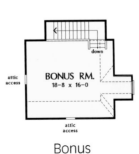

Bonus

Note: Basement floor plans not to scale.

Basement

Rear Elevation

www.basementhomeplans.com

© 2000 Donald A. Gardner, Inc.

MacLachlan
BHPDG01-825D
1-800-388-7580

4 Bedroom, 3 Bath

First Floor	1901 sq ft
Basement	1075 sq ft
Total Living	2976 sq ft
Width	64'0"
Depth	62'4"
Foundation	Hillside Walkout

First Floor

PLAN PRICE SCHEDULE	
	Walkout
1 Set	$660
4 Set	$710
8 Set	$770
Vellum	$990

Note: Basement floor plans not to scale.

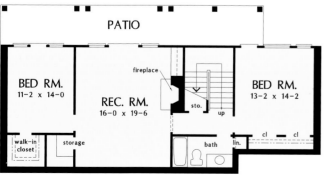

Basement

Rear Elevation

Useful Spaces

© 2002 Donald A. Gardner, Inc.

Oakway
BHPDG01-968A
1-800-388-7580

3 Bedroom, 2 Bath

First Floor............. <u>1470 sq ft</u>
Total Living........... 1470 sq ft
Bonus................... 392 sq ft
Opt. Basement...... 1577 sq ft
Width................... 50'4"
Depth................... 50'0"
Foundation.......... Basement or
                        Crawl Space

PLAN PRICE SCHEDULE		
	Crawl	Basement
1 Set	$525	$750
4 Set	$575	$800
8 Set	$635	$860
Vellum	$795	$1,020

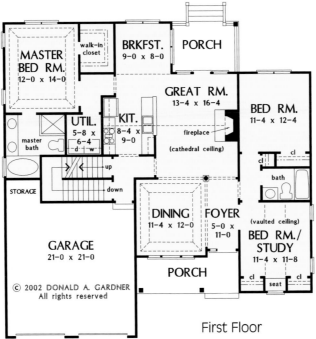

First Floor

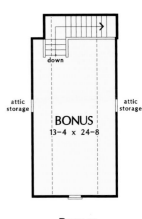

Bonus

Note: Basement floor plans not to scale.

Basement

Rear Elevation

www.basementhomeplans.com

Donald A. Gardner Architect.

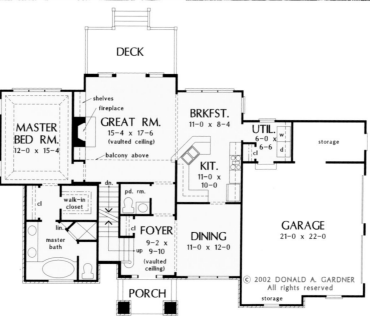

First Floor

© 2002 Donald A. Gardner, Inc.

Luxembourg
BHPDG01-979A
1-800-388-7580

3 Bedroom, 2 1/2 Bath
First Floor............. 1345 sq ft
Second Floor........ 452 sq ft
Total Living........... 1797 sq ft
Bonus.................... 349 sq ft
Opt. Basement...... 1347 sq ft
Width.................... 63'0"
Depth....................40'0"
Foundation...........Basement or
Crawl Space

PLAN PRICE SCHEDULE		
	Crawl	Basement
1 Set	$570	$795
4 Set	$620	$845
8 Set	$680	$905
Vellum	$860	$1,085

Note: Basement floor plans not to scale.

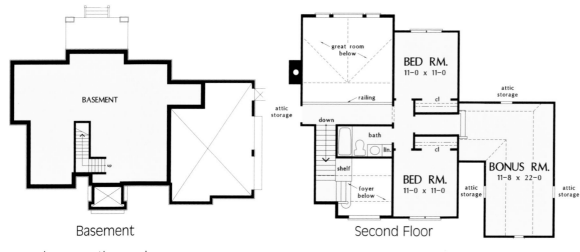

Basement

Second Floor

Rear Elevation

Useful Spaces

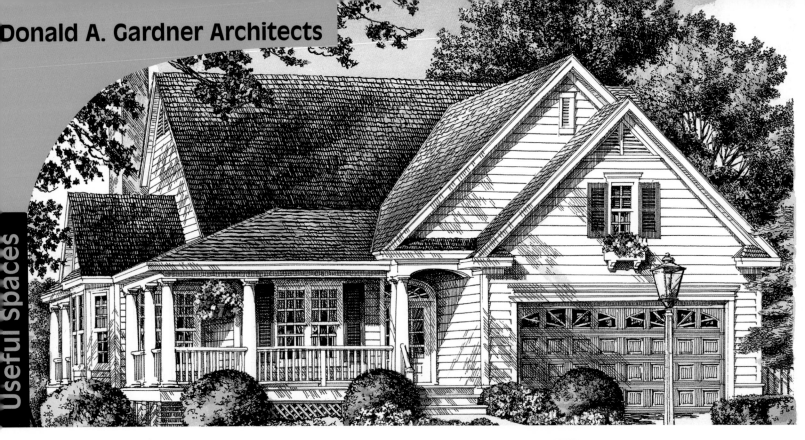

© 2002 Donald A. Gardner, Inc.

Jonesboro
BHPDG01-983A
1-800-388-7580

3 Bedroom, 2 Bath

First Floor............. 1778 sq ft
Total Living........... 1778 sq ft
Bonus.................. 408 sq ft
Opt. Basement...... 1831 sq ft
Width.................. 49'0"
Depth.................. 72'0"
Foundation.......... Basement or Crawl Space

PLAN PRICE SCHEDULE		
	Crawl	Basement
1 Set	$570	$795
4 Set	$620	$845
8 Set	$680	$905
Vellum	$860	$1,085

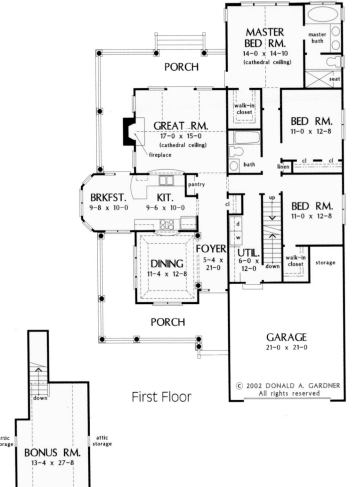

First Floor

Note: Basement floor plans not to scale.

BONUS RM.
13-4 x 27-8

Bonus

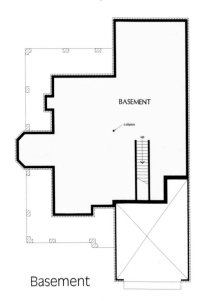

BASEMENT

Basement

Rear Elevation

Useful Spaces

First Floor

PORCH

BRKFST.
13-4 x 14-10

PORCH

UTIL.
9-6 x 5-8

STORAGE

shelves

fireplace

MASTER
BED RM.
14-0 x 17-0

GREAT RM.
20-0 x 17-0

KITCHEN
13-4 x 11-6

up

balcony above

walk-in
closet

lin.

walk-in
closet

walk-in
closet

seat

bath

up

butler's
pantry

GARAGE
22-0 x 22-0

master bath

seat

BED RM./
STUDY
13-4 x 12-0

dn.

balcony
above

FOYER
6-4 x
12-0

DINING
13-4 x 12-0

© 2003 DONALD A. GARDNER
All rights reserved

STORAGE

PORCH

© 2003 Donald A. Gardner, Inc.

Fitzgerald
BHPDG01-1018A
1-800-388-7580

5 Bedroom, 4 Bath

First Floor	2215 sq ft
Second Floor	981 sq ft
Total Living	3196 sq ft
Bonus	402 sq ft
Opt. Basement	2277 sq ft
Width	71'11"
Depth	55'10"
Foundation	Basement or Crawl Space

PLAN PRICE SCHEDULE		
	Crawl	Basement
1 Set	$705	$980
4 Set	$755	$1,030
8 Set	$815	$1,090
Vellum	$1055	$1,330

Note: Basement floor plans not to scale.

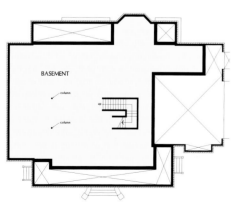

BASEMENT

column

up

column

Basement

shelf

(vaulted ceiling)

BED RM.
13-4 x 12-0
(vaulted ceiling)

attic
storage

attic
storage

great room
below

railing

cl

lin.

lin.

bath

down

attic
storage

attic
storage

BONUS RM.
18-6 x 16-4

walk-in
closet

bath

down

down

railing

attic
storage

BED RM.
13-4 x 12-0

foyer
below

cl

cl

BED RM.
11-0 x 12-0

shelf

Second Floor

Rear Elevation

Donald A. Gardner Architects

© 2004 Donald A. Gardner, Inc.

Fieldstone
BHPDG01-1047A
1-800-388-7580

4 Bedroom, 3 Bath

First Floor.............. <u>2050 sq ft</u>
Total Living............ 2050 sq ft
Bonus.................... 430 sq ft
Opt. Basement...... 2148 sq ft
Width.................... 62'0"
Depth.................... 62'0"
Foundation.......... Basement or
　　　　　　　　 Crawl Space

PLAN PRICE SCHEDULE		
	Crawl	Basement
1 Set	$570	$795
4 Set	$620	$845
8 Set	$680	$905
Vellum	$860	$1,085

Rear Elevation

First Floor

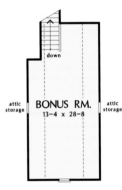

Bonus

Note: Basement floor plans not to scale.

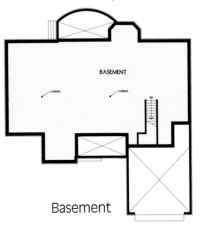

Basement

www.basementhomeplans.com

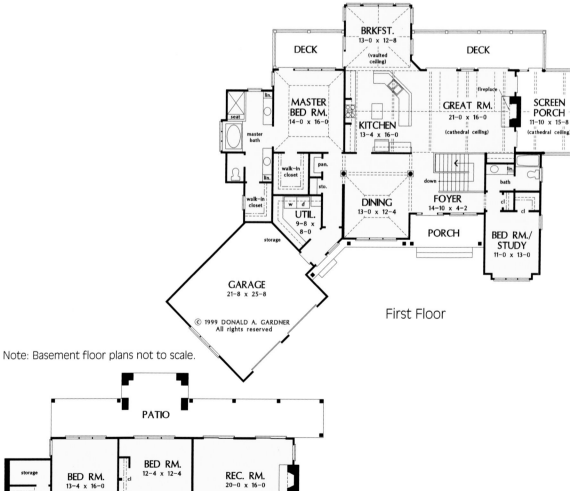

Donald A. Gardner Architects

First Floor

BRKFST.
13-0 x 12-8
(vaulted ceiling)

DECK

DECK

MASTER BED RM.
14-0 x 16-0

seat

master bath

lin.

KITCHEN
13-4 x 16-0

GREAT RM.
21-0 x 16-0
(cathedral ceiling)

fireplace

SCREEN PORCH
11-10 x 15-8
(cathedral ceiling)

walk-in closet

pan.

sto.

walk-in closet

storage

UTIL.
9-8 x 8-0

w d

DINING
13-0 x 12-4

FOYER
14-10 x 4-2

down

bath

lin.

cl

cl

GARAGE
21-8 x 25-8

PORCH

BED RM./ STUDY
11-0 x 13-0

© 1999 DONALD A. GARDNER
All rights reserved

Note: Basement floor plans not to scale.

PATIO

storage

BED RM.
13-4 x 16-0

cl

BED RM.
12-4 x 12-4

REC. RM.
20-0 x 16-0

walk-in closet

bath

lin.

up

sto.

storage

Basement

© 1999 Donald A. Gardner, Inc.

Clairemont
BHPDG01-791D
1-800-388-7580

4 Bedroom, 3 Bath

First Floor............. 2122 sq ft
Basement............. 1150 sq ft
Total Living........... 3272 sq ft
Width.................... 83'0"
Depth.................... 74'4"
Foundation........... Hillside Walkout

PLAN PRICE SCHEDULE	
	Walkout
1 Set	$705
4 Set	$755
8 Set	$815
Vellum	$1,055

Rear Elevation

Each set of Donald A. Gardner plans is a collection of drawings (including components such as floor plans, dimensions, cross sections and elevations) that show you exactly how your house is to be built. Most of our plan packages include:

COVER SHEET

An artist's rendering of the exterior of the house shows you approximately how the house will look when built and landscaped.

FOUNDATION PLAN

This sheet gives the foundation layout, including support walls, excavated and unexcavated areas, if any, and foundation notes. If the foundation is basement rather than monolithic, the plan shows footing and details.

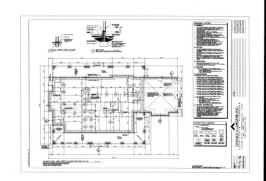

DETAILED FLOOR PLANS

These plans show the layout of each floor of the house. Rooms and interior spaces are carefully dimensioned and keys are given for cross-section details provided later in the plans, as well as window and door size callouts. These plans also show the location of kitchen appliances and bathroom fixtures, as well as suggested locations for electrical fixtures, and outlets.

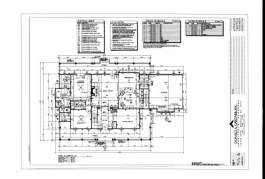

INTERIOR ELEVATIONS/ROOF PLAN

These drawings show the specific details and design of cabinets, utility rooms, fireplaces, bookcases, built-in units and other special interior features depending on the nature and complexity of the item. The roof plan shows the overall layout and necessary details for roof construction. If trusses are used, we suggest using a local truss manufacturer to design your trusses to comply with local codes and regulations.

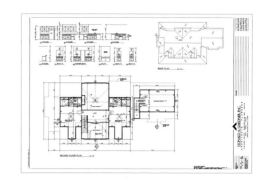

EXTERIOR ELEVATIONS/WALL SECTIONS

Included are front, rear, left and right sides of the house. Exterior materials, details and measurements are also given. This sheet also shows details of the house from the roof to the foundation. This section specifies the home's construction, insulation, flooring and roofing details.

CROSS-SECTION DETAILS

Important changes in floor, ceiling and roof heights or the relationship of one level to another are called out. Also shown, when applicable, are exterior details such as railing and banding.

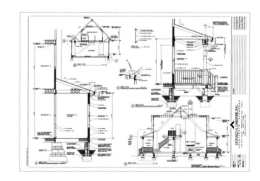

STRUCTURAL PLAN

This sheet gives the overall layout and necessary details for the ceiling, second-floor framing (if applicable) and roof construction.

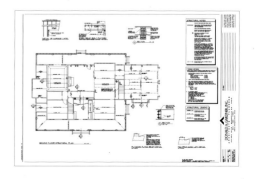

BEFORE YOU ORDER

QUICK TURNAROUND

Because you are placing your order directly to the designer, your plans can be shipped to you quickly. If your order is placed before noon ET, your plans will typically arrive the next business day. Some restrictions may apply. Plans cannot be shipped to a post office box; please provide a physical street address.

EXCHANGE POLICY

Since the designer's blueprints are printed especially for you at the time you place your order, returns are not permitted. If, for some reason, you find that the plan that you purchased does not meet your needs, then you may exchange that plan for another plan in the collection. The designer allows you 60 days from the time of purchase to make an exchange. At the time of the exchange, you will be charged a processing fee of 20 percent of the total amount of the original order plus the difference in price between the plans (if applicable) and the cost to ship the new plans to you. Vellums cannot be exchanged. All sets must be approved and authorization given before the exchange can take place. Please call 1-800-388-7580 if you have any questions.

LOCAL BUILDING CODES AND ZONING REQUIREMENTS

The plans in this book are designed to meet or exceed national building standards. Because of the great differences in geography and climate, each state, county and municipality has its own building codes and zoning requirements. Your plan may need to be modified to comply with local requirements regarding snow loads, energy codes, soil and seismic conditions and a wide range of other matters. Prior to using your plans, the designer strongly advises that you consult a local building official.

ARCHITECTURE AND ENGINEERING SEALS

Some cities and states are now requiring that a licensed architect or engineer review and approve any set of building documents prior to construction. This is due to concern over energy costs, safety, structural integrity and other factors. Prior to applying for a building permit or the start of actual construction, the designer strongly advises that you consult your local building official who can tell you if such a review is required.

DISCLAIMER

The designer has put substantial care and effort into the creation of these plans. The designer authorizes the use of the plans on the express condition that you strictly comply with all local building codes, zoning requirements and other applicable laws, regulations and ordinances. However, because the designer cannot provide on-site consultation, supervision or control over actual construction, and because of the great variance in local building requirements, building practices and soil, seismic, weather and other conditions, THE DESIGNER CANNOT MAKE ANY WARRANTY, EXPRESS OR IMPLIED, WITH RESPECT TO THE CONTENT OR USE OF THE PRINTS OR VELLUMS, INCLUDING BUT NOT LIMITED TO ANY WARRANTY OF MERCHANTABILITY OR OF FITNESS FOR A PARTICULAR PURPOSE.

IGNORING COPYRIGHT LAWS CAN BE A $1,000,000 MISTAKE!

Recent changes in the US copyright laws allow for statutory penalties of up to $150,000 per incident for copyright infringement involving any of the copyrighted plans found in this publication. The law can be confusing. So, for your own protection, take the time to understand what you cannot do when it comes to home plans.

WHAT YOU CAN'T DO!
- You cannot duplicate home plans.
- You cannot copy any part of a home plan to create another.
- You cannot build a home without buying a blueprint or license. Study sets do not include licenses.

How To Order

COPYRIGHT NOTICE

All designs/plans in this publication are protected under the copyright law. Reproduction of the illustrations or working drawings by any means is strictly prohibited. The purchaser of a four-set plan package or greater is licensed to build only one structure from the plans. The purchase of a "study set" stamped "not for construction" does not permit you to construct the house. When purchasing reproducible vellums, the buyer is licensed to build only one structure and reproduce a maximum of 14 sets of plans from the vellums. The designs/plans, in any form, cannot be resold or transferred. Copyright owners may seek full remedies available under the copyright statutes, including statutory damages of up to $150,000 per infringement.

ABOUT OUR PLAN PACKAGE

Plan packages include front rendering, foundation plan, floor plan with electrical fixture layout and plumbing fixtures indicated, exterior and interior elevations, door and window schedules, necessary wall sections/details, structural plan and one specifications outline. Heating/air conditioning layouts are not included. Consult a local mechanical contractor for systems suitable for local climate conditions.

ABOUT BUILDING CODES

At the time of creation, each plan is designed to conform to the CABO One and Two Family Dwelling Code or the International Residential Code. National and local building codes vary with location and change occasionally. Modifications may be necessary to meet local building codes. Consult a builder, architect or other construction professional as necessary. Note: Some states require plans to be sealed and/or re-drawn by a professional architect or engineer licensed in that state. The purchaser is responsible if this requirement applies. Donald A. Gardner Architects, Inc., Donald A. Gardner Design Services, LLC and/or Allora, LLC are not responsible or liable for any changes to the plans, and you accept full responsibility for the accuracy and integrity of any changes or modifications you make.

YOUR BEST VALUE: Reproducible vellums are ideal if you intend to make changes to a design. They allow qualified architects and engineers to modify the design or completely redraw the design per code requirements or personal preference. We recommend you consult the professional making changes before purchasing. The purchaser is permitted to reproduce a maximum of 14 sets of plans from the vellums. If you intend to build a plan more than once, contact our Sales and Support Team at 1-800-388-7580 for more information. Note: To remove the image on the vellum, use either a dark ink eraser in an electric eraser or xerographic eradicator fluid such as Michlin film eradicating fluid applied per manufacturer's directions.

Full reverse plans - Mirror images with correct-reading letters are available for many plans. A materials list aids you in estimating the cost of materials by listing types and quantities of materials needed to build your home.

Square Footage Notes - Total Living square footage is heated square footage, including brick, but not including bonus room square footage (listed separately).

Dimension Notes - Width is defined as the distance from the furthest left point on the exterior wall to the furthest right point on the exterior wall. Depth is defined as the distance from the furthest front point on the exterior wall to the furthest rear point on the exterior wall, including porches, but not including decks or patios.

Call 1.800.388.7580 or Log On to www.basementhomeplans.com

PLAN NUMBER _____

☐ 1 set (study only) ....$ _____

☐ 4-set building package ....$ _____

☐ 8-set building package ....$ _____

☐ 1 set of reproducible vellums ....$ _____

_____ Additional Identical Plans @ $60 each ....$ _____

_____ Full Reverse Plans @ $125 each ....$ _____

Foundation Options: _____

_____ Crawl Space _____ Basement ....$ _____

SUB-TOTAL $ _____

SHIPPING AND HANDLING $ _____

SALES TAX (Will be determined upon placing order) $ _____

TOTAL $ _____

Each Additional Set *Must order within 90 days of original order*	$ 55
Full Reverse Set(s) *Right reading, four-set minimum*	$130
Materials List *List of building materials, estimating tool*	$ 60
Additional Specifications Outline(s) *One outline is included with each plan package purchased*	$ 10

Mini Set *12"x 18" set for reference, min. purchase of 4-set plan pkg. required*	$35
Detached Garage Plans *Call for styles & prices 1-800-388-7580*	

For Modification Services, call (800) 388-7580.

SHIPPING & HANDLING

Overnight	**$40.00**
Priority Overnight	**$50.00**
2nd Day	**$35.00**
Ground	**$20.00**
Saturday (if available)	**$50.00**
International Delivery (Please call for prices & availability.)	

Prices, policies and information subject to change without notice.

INDEX